CW00945873

ARTHUR

AND THE GRAIL

It befell in the days of Uther Pendragon, when he was king of all England, and so reigned, that there was a mighty duke in Cornwall that held war against him long time. And the duke was called the duke of Tintagil. And so by means King Uther sent for this duke, charging him to bring his wife with him, for she was called a fair lady, and a passing wise, and her name was called Igraine.

Sir, said Merlin, this is my desire: the first night that ye shall lie by Igraine ye shall get a child on her, and when that is born, that it shall be delivered to me for to nourish there as I will have it; for it shall be your worship, and the child's avail as mickle as the child is worth.

Design: Bert Willem van der Hout,
Alpha Design, Amsterdam
Lithography: Fotolitomec, Milan/
Edward Lauer, Amsterdam

All photographs in this work are shown as they came out of the camera: no croppings, enlarged details, filters or other tricks were used. The scenes are shown exactly as the photographer saw them through his lens.

The publishers are grateful to
Professional Photo Laboratory
Capi Lux Vak Amsterdam;
Stoomvaart Maatschappij Zeeland;
North Sea Ferries; Townsend Thoresen,
for their co-operation.

First published in Great Britain in 1988
by Sidgwick and Jackson Limited
1 Tavistock Chambers, Bloomsbury Way
London WC1A 2SG

Text © Hubert Lampo 1985
Photography © Pieter Paul Koster 1985
This edition © Sidgwick and Jackson Ltd
1988

Typesetting by Rowland Phototypesetting
Limited
Bury St Edmunds, Suffolk
Printed in Hong Kong

ISBN 0 283 99705 2

Then Sir Bedivere cried: Ah my Lord Arthur, what shall become of me, now ye go from me and leave me here alone among mine enemies? Comfort thyself, said the king, and do as well as thou mayest, for in me is no trust for to trust in; for I will into the vale of Avilion to heal me of my grievous wound: and if thou hear never more of me, pray for my soul.

THOMAS MALORY
Le Morte d'Arthur

But hast Thou not read, O noble gentlemen, answered Don Quixote, the chronicles and histories of England, in which are told the courageous and heroic deeds of King Arthur . . . saying he never died . . . and that in time he would reign again, and regain his kingdom and his sceptre.

MIGUEL DE CERVANTES
Don Quixote

Well, said Merlin, I know a lord of yours in this land, that is a passing true man and a faithful, and he shall have the nourishing of your child, and his name is Sir Ector, and he is a lord of fair livelihood in many parts in England and Wales . . .

Dedicated to Laurens Van Krevelen

HUBERT LAMPO

In honour of Gerard Lutz

PIETER PAUL KOSTER

4

Acknowledgements

I wish to take this opportunity of paying my respects to the late Valeer Van Kerkhove, chief producer of Flemish Television, who asked me to write the television documentary 'In the Footsteps of King Arthur' in 1981. The work involved in this project renewed my interest in the subject and inspired me to write a book on Arthur. My thanks also to photographer Pieter Paul Koster and publisher Gerlag van Gendt, who both encouraged me to write this work. I should not want to forget to thank my once and future publisher of Meulenhoff-Nederland, Laurens Van Krevelen, for his generous permission to reproduce my essay on Arthur. Furthermore I am grateful to all the authors mentioned in the bibliography, without whose research and knowledge this work would not have been possible. My special thanks to Professor Jean Markele, and to Geoffrey Ashe, who was instrumental in making the above-mentioned documentary on Arthur. Last, but not least, I should like to thank sincerely my friend Colin Wilson, who agreed without hesitation to write the introduction to this book.

HUBERT LAMPO

C O N T E N T S

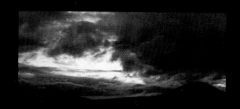

INTRODUCTION

On Sunday, 16 August 1924, that remarkable visionary Rudolf Steiner visited 'King Arthur's Castle' at Tintagel, in Cornwall, and was so deeply impressed that he devoted most of a lecture to the Arthur legend the following Friday in Torquay. His secretary and biographer Güenther Wachsmuth was with him, and he records how Steiner pointed to various places in the ruins, identifying them as the hall of the Round Table, the sleeping quarters of the knights and so on. In his Torquay lecture, Steiner described how, as he stood looking over the sea, watching the 'wonderful interplay between the light and the air', he saw with the 'eyes of the spirit' the truth about the great mission of King Arthur and his knights.

It is an impressive lecture; for the modern reader, it has only the slight disadvantage of being pure imagination. For we are in a position to know that the castle at Tintagel was not in existence during the lifetime of the British general Artorius, who lived from about AD 470 to 540; the castle was built about six centuries later, around AD 1140. In the days of King Arthur – or General Artorius – there was only a Celtic monastery on the site.

Even so, what Steiner had to say about Arthur was fascinating in itself, and in some respects echoes the arguments of the present book. The Archangel Michael, he says, is a 'sun spirit', whose task is to bring about 'a more esoteric understanding of the truths of Christianity'. For, according to Steiner, Christ also came from the sun, which is also the source of intelligence. Arthur's task was to become the vessel of the sun-forces working in nature at Tintagel, and to cause these forces to spread all over Europe, much of it still dominated by the 'wild demonic powers of old'. A group of twelve men surrounded Arthur, as the constellations of the zodiac are grouped around the sun. This grouping, says Steiner, is the symbolic 'Round Table', a circle of the twelve knights, with Arthur at the centre. Their mission was to set out on expeditions throughout Europe, to carry the forces of civilization – the sun-force – to all the dark places.

It would be a mistake to dismiss Steiner as a crank. Anyone who reads the *Autobiography* will recognize that he is a man of keen intelligence and immense erudition. And there are many stories of his remarkable spiritual and psychological insight. Such a man is no charlatan. Then how do we explain his preposterous statements about Tintagel castle? The answer may be that, like all highly gifted 'psychics', he was often unable to distinguish between genuine 'paranormal' insights and dream-like visions originating in the unconscious mind. Steiner seems to have possessed to a very high degree the

So on the morn all the barons with Merlin came before the king; then Merlin said aloud unto King Uther, Sir, shall your son Arthur be king after your days, of this realm with all the appurtenance? Then Uther Pendragon turned him, and said in hearing of them all, I give him God's blessing and mine . . .

power that Jung called 'active imagination', which is virtually the ability to dream with the eye open. It could also be startlingly accurate. On that same trip to Great Britain, Steiner and Wachsmuth visited prehistoric stone circles in Wales, and Steiner told Wachsmuth that they were built as a kind of astronomical calculator – a theory put forward about 40 years later by Professor Gerald Hawkins (it is described in this book). He went on to explain in some detail how the ancient priests used the stone circle, and hills and depressions on the horizon, to work out the cosmic rhythms that determined the spiritual festivals – thereby anticipating the later researches of Professor Alexander Thom.

Whether or not his visions at Tintagel were pure imagination, it seems clear that Steiner had recognized that wider, semi-mythical significance of King Arthur that Hubert Lampo investigates in this erudite but immensely readable book – a book that is, in my own opinion, the best general introduction ever written on this immensely complex subject.

Hubert Lampo, born in 1920, is one of the most distinguished and widely read writers on the continent of Europe. Born in Antwerp (where he still lives), Lampo achieved fame while still in his early twenties with novels which, according to one commentator, stand astride 'the expressionistic-vitalistic and the realistic-psychological currents'. In the Netherlands his name is always associated with the phrase 'magical realism', and this in turn sheds a great deal of light on his attitude to King Arthur. Lampo explained his 'magical realism' to me as follows:

'My novel *The Return of Joachim Stiller* was conceived as an ordinary realistic novel, but while it was being written, and contrary to the author's plans, more and more unreal elements emerged, culminating in the appearance of one Joachim Stiller near the end of the book. He is a sort of Messianic figure whose death and disappearance from the mortuary deliver the novel's protagonists from their incertitudes and fears. As an absolute unbeliever, I found an explanation of the appearance of the 'Christ-like' figure in C. G. Jung. In order to free himself as well as his characters of their fears, the author, while writing the novel, had unconsciously come under the spell of what Jung calls the Messianic archetype.

'The discovery of such archetypal content in his own work furnished me with the key which I needed to prove that a number of more or less fantastic authors (Rider Haggard, Arthur Machen, H. P. Lovecraft, John Cowper Powys, John Fowles, Meyrink, Kafka, Alain-Fournier, Borges, Dinu Buzatti and others – a mixed lot indeed) do not just draw upon a wild and nonsensical imagination, but write from the source of Jung's collective unconscious. They organically incorporate the archetypes which potentially reside in the collective unconscious into concrete reality, and in this fashion melt together dream and reality into one indissoluble whole. Apart from purely literary and poetical qualities, their great impact on the public is attributable to the fact that they address readers at the level of their participation in the collective unconscious. In my study *The Swans of Stonehenge* I preferred to call this type of literature magical realism . . .'

Lampo had always been interested in King

And when matins and the first mass was done, there was seen in the churchyard, against the high altar, a great stone four square, like unto a marble stone, and in midst thereof was like an anvil of steel a foot on high, and therein stuck a fair sword naked by the point, and letters there were written in gold about the sword that said thus:– Whoso pulleth out this sword of this stone and anvil, is rightwise king born of all England.

Arthur – ever since, as a child in Antwerp, he read Wolfram von Eschenbach's *Parzival*, in which Parsifal's son Lohengrin comes to Antwerp to protect the Duchess of Brabant from her enemies, and marries her. Antwerp is a fascinating old city, and its cathedral is the most beautiful in Europe; for the young Lampo, reading about Lohengrin must have felt like becoming a part of a medieval myth. (When I visited the city in 1982 with my wife, he showed us around the part of the old town where the story of Lohengrin is set.) As a youth, he also became familiar with Wagner's *Lohengrin*, which was part of the repertoire of the Royal Flemish Opera. So when, in 1980, he was asked to write and narrate a television programme on King Arthur, it was simply a return to a subject that had always touched his imagination. He travelled around England with a television crew, studying all the famous Arthurian sites, including Tintagel, which is only an hour from where I live. He and his wife called on me on that occasion, and we discussed the legends, about which I had also written. At that time, I told him about a friend of mine, the late Dr Harold Phelps, who was engaged in writing a book claiming that King Arthur never existed. We were united in our feeling that such a theory is finally untenable; nothing seems less likely than that the legends of King Arthur are a case of smoke without fire.

Yet Harold Phelps's theory is not wholly unreasonable. If Arthur existed, he was an Anglo-Roman general who organized the resistance against the Saxon invaders who eventually overran the British Isles, and who won a dozen major victories over them, the last and greatest of these being a certain battle of Badon. A document called the *Easter Annals*, written

soon after the time of Arthur, refers to him as the hero of the battle of Badon, and two centuries later, a monk called Nennius listed the 12 battles fought by Arthur. But it was around 1135 – when England was under the harsh Norman yoke – that a chronicler called Geoffrey of Monmouth wrote his preposterous *History of the Kings of Britain*, telling the story of how Arthur was born in Tintagel castle after the magician Merlin had transformed King Uther Pendragon so he looked like the husband of Igerne. Geoffrey also tells incredible tales of Arthur's conquests that make him one of the greatest empire builders since Julius Caesar. It was after Geoffrey of Monmouth's book that the King Arthur legends snowballed, and he became one of the most popular heroes in European history. The Arthur later described by Malory is essentially a medieval knight who bears no resemblance to the real Arthur, who undoubtedly wore Roman armour and carried a Roman short sword. In *that* sense, King Arthur is a myth. But why did that myth achieve such a hold on the imagination of Europe?

For a long time, I was inclined to accept the commonsense explanation. There *was* an Arthur legend long before Geoffrey of Monmouth, as Lampo shows in the opening chapter of his book, and its potency derived from the folk-belief that Arthur was still alive, and would return one day to lead the British against foreign invaders. This legend, as Lampo says, may have arisen because Arthur's death was originally kept a secret. The Normans, who invaded England in 1066, were exceptionally harsh masters; they treated the Saxons as badly as the Romans had treated the original Britons nine centuries earlier. The legend of the return of Arthur kept hope alive,

And at the feast of Pentecost all manner of men essayed to pull at the sword that would essay, but none might prevail but Arthur, and pulled it out afore all the lords and commons that were there, wherefore all the commons cried at once, We will have Arthur unto our king, we will put him no more in delay, for we all see that it is God's will that he shall be our king, and who that holdeth against it, we will slay him.

much as General de Gaulle's broadcasts from London kept alive the hope of the French Resistance in the Second World War. The 'Arthur phenomenon' was, in many respects, similar to the *Lord of the Rings* phenomenon of the 1960s, when every literate teenager knew the book by heart, and there were daubed signs in the London Underground reading 'Gandalf Lives!'. It was an 'escapist' myth of enormous potency.

Of course, *The Lord of the Rings* was written by one man, and the Arthurian legends by many. But that makes no fundamental difference. The point is, surely, that in a time when reality was all too grim and hard, the King Arthur legends presented a vision of some delightful past age when everything was somehow more beautiful and exciting. We should also remember that the period of the Arthur legends corresponds roughly with the early period of the 'witch craze' in Europe, with everyone suddenly obsessed by thoughts of magic spells and evil (but often beautiful) women having intercourse with demons; the Arthur legends echo all this. In short, the story of Arthur was a kind of ideal melting pot into which all the contemporary poets and romancers could pour their dreams and nightmares. A few centuries later, the legend of Robin Hood served the same purpose – with its basic outline of a man who turns his back on the towns and the tax collectors, and lives in the forest with his 'merry men', dining off the king's venison. But Robin was never quite so suitable as Arthur; his story contains no wicked enchanters, no incestuous half-sisters, no adulterous queens. No story exercised such a hold on the European imagination until the birth of the Faust legend in the late fifteenth century.

This was my own explanation of the popularity of the Arthur legends – until I came to read Jessie L. Weston's book *The Legend of Sir Lancelot du Lac*. In this work, she has a chapter on the tale of Sir Lancelot and the white-footed stag, in which a beautiful maiden appears at Arthur's court and asks for a hero to go and kill seven lions that are guarding a white-footed stag; she says she will give her hand to the hero who brings her the stag's foot. Sir Lancelot accomplishes the mission, but is so sorely wounded that, when a stranger knight rides by, he asks him to take the stag's foot back to Arthur's court, and to send help. The stranger knight treacherously attacks Lancelot and leaves him for dead, then rides back to court to claim the hand of the lady. Queen Guinevere instinctively dislikes him, and delays the marriage; meanwhile, Gawain sets out in search of Lancelot, finds him half dead, and gets him to a hermit who tends his wounds. The two knights arrive back at court just in time to prevent the marriage, and Lancelot slays the treacherous knight. However, he declines the hand of the lady, on the grounds that all his devotion is to Guinevere.

Miss Weston points out that this is a thoroughly unsatisfactory ending, and that there are other curious inconsistencies in the tale – for example, how Gawain succeeds in finding Lancelot with nothing to guide him. But she unearthed an earlier tale called *Tyolet* which is altogether more satisfactory; in this story, the lady arrives at court with a brachet hound, and the hound accompanies Tyolet on his quest; when Tyolet is wounded by the treacherous knight, it is the hound that returns to court and guides Gawain to Tyolet. Finally, Tyolet weds the maiden, after slaying the treacherous knight.

Then he drew his sword Excalibur, but it was so bright in his enemies' eyes, that it gave light like thirty torches.

Obviously, says Professor Weston, *Tyolet* was the original version of the tale, and it was later transferred to Lancelot because he was the more popular hero. It is basically a version of the popular medieval legend of the false claimant, in which someone tries to pass himself off as the hero, but is found out. And she points out that one of the earliest versions of the false claimant legend is a story in which Perseus kills a dragon, and removes its tongue as well as its head; the false claimant is revealed to be a cheat because he does not know about the removal of the tongue.

This seems to show conclusively that it is a mistake to think of the Arthur legends as being a kind of late medieval counterpart of *The Lord of the Rings*. The poets and balladeers did not invent; they retold ancient myths and legend, transforming them in the process.

One of the first investigators to take myths seriously was Sir James Fraser, whose original two volumes of *The Golden Bough* appeared in 1890. Frazer was inclined to regard all myths as having their origin in fertility rituals, attempts to influence the gods to guarantee a good harvest. His work was eventually expanded to 13 large volumes. Yet, oddly enough, he had little or nothing to say about the Arthur legends. Jessie L. Weston remedied this in her book *From Ritual to Romance* (1920), which traced the Grail legend to fertility rituals; in short, she asserted that such myths form a link between sex and religion. T. S. Eliot was greatly influenced by the book, and took his title *The Waste Land* from its second chapter.

In the present book, Hubert Lampo has gone one step further still, and linked the Arthur legends with Jung's theory of the archetypes of the collective unconscious. Jung first formulated this theory in about 1911, as a deliberate counterblast to Freud's belief that the unconscious roots of human behaviour – and culture – lie in sex; Jung was trying to 'de-sexualize' psychology, and he was almost certainly influenced by Frazer, whose *Golden Bough* is, virtually, a theory of archetypes.

Lampo argues his case very persuasively, and he certainly has me more than half convinced. And if I have certain reservations, it is only because I have myself written a book about Jung that demanded an exhaustive study of his work, and ended with a great many unresolved doubts. Jung's reputation stands very high at the moment, for the breadth of his vision seems so much wider than Freud's. I had originally intended to write a very large book about him, an exhaustive study of his ideas, but for various reasons, the project was delayed; in the meantime, I agreed to write a shorter work about Jung for another publisher. As I settled down to the enormous task of reading his collected works, I became increasingly relieved that I had not signed the contract to write the larger work. When Jung became a disciple and defender of Freud, he turned his back on the older type of 'phenomenological' psychology represented by Pierre Janet. Freud's sexual theory seemed so much more daring and exciting. Within four years, Jung had decided he could not stomach Freud's insistence that *all* mental illness has its origin in sex. 'The soul possesses by nature a religious function,' he was to say later. In *Transformation and Symbols of the Libido* (1911) he paid lip service to Freud, but insisted that religious and mythical symbols play a basic part in man's unconscious life. When I actually read the book, I found it unconvincing; it looked more

So after the feast and journey, King Arthur drew him unto London, and so by the counsel of Merlin, the king let call his barons to council, for Merlin had told the king that the six kings that made war upon him would in all haste be awroke on him and on his lands.

like an attempt to 'upstage' Freud than a genuine attempt to discover deeper truths about the unconscious. I was also profoundly disturbed by Jung's attitude towards the 'occult'; he admits in his autobiography *Memories, Dreams, Reflections* that he was fully aware of the reality of the 'paranormal' from an early age; yet until late in life he kept insisting that it could all be explained away in terms of the unconscious mind – he was obviously worried about his reputation as a 'scientist'. It was only after a serious illness and a 'near death experience' at 68 that he decided to 'come clean'. I was also disturbed by his theories about alchemy; they seemed, frankly, to be based upon appalling ignorance of the European magical tradition – so that he again tries to explain in terms of the 'archetypes of the collective unconscious' things that any student of magic could have explained much more straightforwardly. In short, I came to feel that Jung is a bit of a charlatan and a bit of a fool. A great man, certainly – but not the profound sage that his disciples seem to take him for.

So I confess that when it comes to interpreting the Arthur myths in Jungian terms, I began to experience a certain resistance; I suspect that in 50 years time, we shall have discounted about 50 per cent of what Jung has to say about the collective unconscious.

But as I read Lampo's immensely scholarly and yet at the same time marvellously readable study of King Arthur, these reservations seem relatively unimportant. What he has done, it seems to me, is to create a worthy companion to his remarkable novel *The Return of Joachim Stiller*, a powerful and moving example of 'magical realism'. The 'realism' lies in the scholarship, in his immensely wide erudition about the Arthurian literature; yet the shaping force of the book is his powerful imagination, which seems to completely at home in the bleak wastes around Dozmary Pool (where the Lady of the Lake is said to have received the sword Excalibur), or in the enchanted countryside around Glastonbury. The author uses the themes of Arthur scholarship as if they were musical themes, to create his own Arthur Symphony. If Rutland Boughton – the creator of an epic series of operas about Arthur – were still alive, he would have recognized a fellow spirit in Hubert Lampo.

COLIN WILSON

1. THE BODMIN INCIDENT

And through the wit of Merlin, he led the host northward, the priviest way that could be thought, unto the forest of Bedegraine, and there in a valley he lodged them secretly.

On a summer's day in the year of Our Lord 1113, the small town of Bodmin in Cornwall was roused from its provincial slumber by the arrival of an impressive band of French clerics. The population was overwhelmed by a sense of excitement. One of the monks was an Englishman, Robert, from whom the gathering crowd learned what was afoot. The full story can be read in the Chronicle of Herman de Tournai, the *Miracula Sanctae Mariae Laudunensies* (1193).

The company had come from Laon in France, where a year earlier the church had been seriously damaged by fire during a popular revolt. The canons of the Chapter of Notre Dame immediately decided to set out on a fund-raising tour to collect the necessary means to build a new place of worship. They took with them the shrine containing the wonderful relics of the Holy Virgin. After a journey through northwestern France, the company embarked at Wissant (Pas de Calais) and arrived in Dover after a stormy crossing. After visiting Canterbury, the clergymen travelled resolutely west. Every so often, the shrine was exhibited. Both the expected miracles (that on occasion seemed to stem from the medical knowledge of the travellers) and the generous donations were numerous. The visitors were regularly offered money, jewels, rich fabrics, gold and objects worked in previous metals.

In Exeter, the priests were told that they would soon reach the land of King Arthur. When they arrived in Cornwall, they were struck, while crossing the moors, by the prehistoric stone constructions, two of which were known to the local population as Arthur's Seat and Arthur's Oven and were famous in the stories from Britain. The constructions in question were most likely the present Arthur's Bed, a granite monolith, and Arthur's Hall, a rectangular construction of the same material, with no recognizable purpose.

The company finally reached Bodmin, where it had been decided to exhibit the relics in order to give the population a chance to take advantage of their healing powers. The impressive shrine was set up and an incident occurred between the crowds of faithful and a servant of the priests, a certain Haganellus. One of the locals had been speaking to him excitedly about King Arthur, adding that he was still alive, only to be told by the apparently irritable Frenchman that he was talking nonsense. Much to the amazement of the clerics from Laon, this denial caused great indignation among the simple and pious souls gathered round the shrine. Several armed Cornishmen immediately burst into the church with the obvious intention of teaching the sceptical foreigners a lesson. And had Algardus, the monk's leader, not come between them, it is likely the incident would have ended in

The king with the hundred knights met a wonder dream two nights afore the battle, that there blew a great wind, and blew down their castles and their *towns, and after that came a water and bare it all away. All that heard of the sweven, said it was a token of great battle.*

And they set on them fiercely in the passage, and slew on the right hand and on the left hand that it was wonder to tell.

bloodshed, at least according to Herman de Tournai. A few conclusions may be drawn from what appears at first sight to be no more than an unimportant, rather comical anecdote.

In 1113 a number of tales centring around a certain King Arthur were circulating among the British population. The inhabitants of Cornwall were not only convinced that he really existed, but also apparently believed that he was still alive. From Haganellus' denial, it follows that Arthur was in no way unknown to him, yet he refused to accept that Arthur may not have been dead. There is nothing in de Tournai's chronicle to indicate that the French clergymen seriously questioned the tales about Arthur; it was his centuries' long lifespan they found hard to believe. We can safely assume that they were sufficiently aware of what in their day was considered current religious literature. A number of British saints' lives dating back to 1100 or shortly after have been preserved in which Arthur, for quite astonishing reasons, features as a protagonist. There are the – in this context somewhat late perhaps – *Life of Saint Gildas* by the Welshman Caradoc of Llancarfan, and two anonymous texts, the *Life of Saint Carannog* and the *Life of Saint Padernus*.

In the first book we learn that Arthur killed the brother of Gildas, a certain Hueil. In the second, it is said that he stole a precious altar from the prelate Carannog and used it blasphemously as a dining table. Thirdly, Padernus also fell victim to Arthur's audacity when he was robbed of a tunic that was considered a relic and had been given to him by the patriarch of Jerusalem. On three occasions, our man turns out to be a scoundrel. As has already been pointed out, it is safe to assume that the French priests were familiar with

books of that kind. Gildas' biography may have appeared somewhat too late in this respect but, since he was held in great veneration in Brittany, there is a fair chance that the French priests had at least heard the legends that gave rise to his life story. In any case, it is almost certain that they knew of King Arthur, because Herman situates him in 'the stories of Britain', which can also be understood to mean continental Brittany. As sons of the church they had, however, ample reason to deny to such an unprincipled thief and sacrilegious cut-throat the lifespan of a biblical patriarch.

Nowhere in the *Miracula Sanctae Mariae Laudunensies* is there an indication that the inhabitants of Bodmin in 1113 were aware that Arthur was in the clergy's black books. On the other hand, it is a fact that he was remembered in English religious circles as a fierce warrior who, in his relations with the monastic communities of his time, was apparently not in the habit of handling matters with kid gloves.

However little the monks – who put the lives of the saints down in writing – may have thought of Arthur, the fact remains that it is their texts that seem to provide us with fairly convincing psychological evidence of his veracity as a historical character. The fact is that, 600 years after the crimes attributed to him had been committed, it would have been quite natural for the clergy to adapt to the contemporary view of someone who, in the course of the intervening centuries, had been promoted by popular imagination into a soldier, a leader in the war against the heathen Saxons and a true knight. However, the scribes of the year 1100 or thereabouts, apparently indifferent as to their credibility with a public ignorant of the facts of

*Then Sir Arthur did so
marvellously in arms, that all
men had wonder.*

Then waxed the battle passing hard on both parties, but Arthur was glad that his knights were horsed again, and then they fought together, that the noise and sound rang by the water and the wood.

history and who had long regarded Arthur as a demigod, made no use at all of the possibilities offered them in terms of propaganda by such a famous character. It seems as though, in the abbeys, the memory of a historically genuine character had been retained through centuries – a character whose unchristian deeds the servants of God refused to condone, however popular he might have been with ordinary men and women.

This digression on the Bodmin incident and the mention of the British lives of the saints is primarily related to the much debated problem of whether Arthur may or may not be considered as a historical character. As far as I can see, too little attention has been paid to the psychological factor in works of that nature. By this I mean the inopportune nature of a purely negative Arthur profile at a time when the people regarded him as a hero who could do no wrong. In the meantime, further investigation is necessary to reveal the elements tending to support the view that the King Arthur who is very much a mythical product was actually a man of flesh and blood.

Without really going into detail at this stage, we can start off by saying that Arthur largely belongs to the Celtic world.

Of Indo-European stock, originating from an area situated near the upper course of the Danube and Rhine, the Celts seem to have been seized by something like a westward urge as early as the second millennium BC. In the eighth and ninth centuries BC, the Celts constituted the population of Great Britain, albeit mingled with the earlier inhabitants. They lived in tribal communities which led to the creation of small kingdoms. A king-chief ruled over each kingdom and commanded his own small army, a kind of private militia made up of members of the higher classes, a fact which at this stage seems already to presage the later knights of the Round Table. Professional poets, the bards, were held in high esteem and sang the heroic deeds of the leader and his companions. Agriculture and stock-breeding began to play an important part in the lives of the Celts when they adopted a settled way of life. Their astonishing mobility had earlier been greatly enhanced by their horse-drawn vehicles, which were buried with persons of high rank, as can be seen at the burial site of a princess in Vix in Burgundy. Their settlements were often strategically situated hill-forts; these are – even now – easily recognizable and impressive structures built on the hillsides and hilltops of the English countryside. The settlements were also economic centres where skilled craftsmen, often gifted artists, carried on their trade.

Julius Caesar, in his *De Bello Gallico*, talks about *druides*, *equites* and *plebs*, i.e. the druids, the warriors and the 'common' folk. The druids form a separate professional caste of intellectuals, scholars and priests. Comparable in a way to the Indian Brahmans, their existence corresponds to an ancient Indo-European cultural tradition. The sum total of their – possibly somewhat dubious – knowledge is contained in endless verses, never committed to writing. They possess a great knowledge of the stars and their movements, the dimensions of the universe and the earth, the philosophy of nature, the powers and provinces of the eternal gods. In fact, little is known of their conceptions of man and the unknown. Classical writers point out that the Celts believed the soul to be eternal. The fact is that a considerable number of Celtic tales are centred round the journey to another paradise

But when Sir Arthur saw the
battle would not be ended by no
the left hand, that he stinted not
till he had slain twenty knights

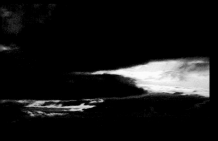

All these knights rode on afore with spears on their thighs, and spurred their horses mightily as the horses might run.

world situated underground or over the sea, where the dead, together with the gods, spirits, fairies and other mythical beings, lead an eternal and particularly pleasant existence.

However much Arthur may come across as the last hero of the Celtic world, he also bears the mark of the four centuries of Roman rule which preceded his appearance.

Twice in two successive years, in 55 and 54 BC, Julius Caesar attempted in vain to land on the coast of Britain. A discreet memorial plaque on the seafront in Walmer in Kent reminds the present-day tourist of these unsuccessful attempts. The emperor Claudius was more successful in AD 43. He secured a bridgehead in the vicinity of Sandwich where he established his base of Rutupiae, now Richborough, whose impressive remains can be visited today. In the space of four years the entire south was in Roman hands, followed later by Wales. In AD 61 a revolt broke out among the Iceni, led by the widowed Queen Boadicea who, after having been raped together with her daughters, took her revenge in the apocalyptic slaughter of Romans, razed London and St Albans to the ground, but was finally defeated and committed suicide. Her spirit now roams Epping Forest but her grave is in London where, according to tradition, you have to look for it under platform 10 at King's Cross Station.

After being taken over by the empire, a new and prosperous period opened up for the Britons.

Soon fine Roman roads linked every part of the country. They can still be clearly seen today in many lovely spots, as attractive paved footpaths through the unspoiled countryside. 'Modern' towns grew up, designed on the drawing-board by experienced town planners. The countryside

was soon sprinkled with villas, mainly farming estates at first, but later luxurious country houses whose remains, beautifully conserved by the current authorities, bear witness to the high living standard of the Romano-British population. Carefully groomed gentlemen and extravagantly attired ladies visited Aqua Sulis – now Bath – the fashionable spa, whose wonderful bathing facilities could very well be used even today. The gold, silver, tin, lead and iron mines supported a flourishing export trade, while luxury goods were imported from the Mediterranean area.

Druidism, considered subversive, was ruthlessly stamped out but old local gods were generally tolerated and were worshipped by the native and even by part of the Romanized poulation. Many soldiers who were not exclusively Roman offered prayers to Mithras, whose cult had originated in Persia and whose temples have been unearthed in many different places. Christianity also gained ground in Britain, especially after 313, when Constantine the Great made it the official creed of the empire. Set in the beautiful mosaic floor of the villa at Hinton St Mary is the oldest beardless representation of Christ of the Roman period, while the Chi Rho monogram in the villa of Lullingstone in Kent is clear evidence of early Christianization.

The prosperous days of the *Pax Romana* were, however, soon to come to an end. We know that, as early as the end of the third century, the admiral of the Roman fleet, Marcus Aurelius Carausius, a Menapian from Flanders who in 286 was proclaimed emperor by his troops, was forced to wage an uninterrupted war against Frankish and Saxon pirates. He lived in Britain but was murdered in Boulogne, Pas de Calais, in

With that came Merlin on a great
black horse, and said unto
Arthur, Thou hast never done,
hast thou not done enough? of
three score thousand this day hast
thou left alive but fifteen
thousand, and it is time to say
Ho!

And there had Arthur the first sight of Guenever, the king's daughter of Cameliard, and ever after he loved her. After they were wedded . . .

more frequent. The situation became really disastrous on the Continent in 406 when the Franks crossed the frozen Rhine in large numbers and overran the province of Gaul. Around 410, the Romans were forced to withdraw their troops from Britain. The Britons were officially informed that, from then on, they would have to ensure the country's defence alone. The southeast slowly fell into the hands of the barbaric, heathen Saxons, Angles, Jutes and Friesians, who destroyed what remained of the British Roman culture, camped like gypsies among the ruins of the villas and stamped out every trace of early Christianity.

The representatives of the ruling classes may still have seen themselves as Romans but they unfortunately lacked the Romans' central administration, numerical strength and strategic insight. The struggle against the Germanic invaders was pursued through changing fortunes under the leadership of the Celtic chief Vortigern, who dissociated himself from the lingering Roman influence. Vortigern had not only to stand his ground against the Saxons, but had also to deal with the Picts swarming in through the north of Scotland. In an attempt to conciliate these awe-inspiring barbarians, Vortigern made a mistake: he granted a number of Saxons free access to the country on condition that they join the British troops as mercenaries. He had in fact chosen the lesser of two evils but, when the Saxons broke their word, it was clear that he had brought in a Trojan horse. Despite his good intentions, he came to be regarded as the arch-traitor in the early history of Great Britain.

After his death in 460, Ambrosius Aureliarus, a Romanized Briton for whom the imperial dream had remained very much alive, rose to power.

The Britons at that time were divided by a long-standing political struggle between what we would call the Celtic nationalists and the supporters of Rome. The latter enjoyed the support of the church whose sympathies, likewise, lay with imperial Rome. Furthermore, the position of the church had emerged strengthened from the conflict, settled in her favour, with the heretical, though popular, doctrine of Pelagius (350–426), a layman according to some, a monk from Wales or Brittany according to others. Pelagius had questioned original sin as well as the Christian doctrine of divine grace and had found strong support in Vortigern and his followers. The orthodox Catholic Ambrosius Aurelianus was driven by memories of what the glorious Roman golden age had meant for members of his caste. Moreover, he was kept buoyant by the thought that his country was still part of the empire, the withdrawal of the legions merely being regarded as an annoying technical detail. It was no more than an illusion, but one that bore fruit. When he left the scene, the struggle against the Germanic invaders was continued efficiently. Around 520, the Saxons suffered serious defeat, holding them in check for a long time to come; some of them even returned to the Continent.

There are reasons to believe that the leader of the decisive battle was Arthur.

*So they were agreed, and he
begat upon her Mordred, and she
was his sister, on his mother's
side, Igraine. So there she rested
her a month, and at the last
departed.*

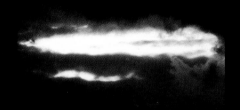

2. ARTHUR: LEGEND OR REALITY?

Thus was the dream of Arthur: Him thought there was come into this land griffins and serpents, and him thought they burnt and slew all the people in the land, and then him thought he fought with them, and they did him passing great harm, and wounded him full sore, but at the last he slew them.

Much later, in the twelfth and thirteenth centuries, King Arthur appears as the hero of a number of pseudo-historical and purely literary works. Prior to this period, mention of his name is strikingly rare but not altogether imaginary.

The main source for the study of this period is the *De Excidio et Conquesta Britanniae* (*The Downfall and Conquest of Britain*) of around 840. The author of this work is the cleric Gildas, who died in 570 and whose biography has already been mentioned. Unhappy with the political, religious and moral state of affairs in his native land, he left for Rhuys in Brittany where, fleeing from the approaching Saxons, a large number of Britons had already settled, bringing their traditions with them. *De Excidio*, described by Gildas himself as his 'Book of Lamentations', gives a general view of British history, painting a bitter picture of the downfall of the earlier Roman grandeur and of the deplorable way in which local rulers from Wales and Cornwall administer the affairs of the country. It is, however, very disappointing that Gildas, the angry old man, should never once mention Arthur's name, even though he is talking about historical facts in which, according to tradition, Arthur must have played a prominent part. These facts mainly relate to the battle of Mons Badonicus, Mount Badon, where the Saxon advance was thoroughly beaten back.

Some historians believe that Gildas' silence need not necessarily be construed as evidence that Arthur was a purely imaginary character. The *De Excidio* contains conspicuously few exact topographical details or proper names. It must be remembered that Gildas' lamentations were quite clearly aimed at his contemporaries, in an attempt to convince them that they should share his own fierce indignation. Transposing the problem to our own day and age, it is possible to imagine that an author writing about the Battle of the Bulge might not necessarily mention the name of General Patton. Moreover, there may be another reason for Gildas' silence where the glorious leader at Mount Badon is concerned. We remember the shocking fact in the previously mentioned Caradoc of Llancarfan's *Vita Gildae*, that the holy man's brother – in reality probably a traitor collaborating with the Saxons – had been killed by Arthur. Bearing in mind that Gildas is certainly not one for forgiving easily, it would make sense, psychologically, to assume that he would remain fanatically silent about both his arch-enemy and his none too innocent brother. Finally, there is the question of Arthur's attitude to religion. If Arthur's sympathies lay with the old Celtic church whose views in many respects differed from those of Rome, then the orthodox Gildas could hardly be expected to appreciate the fact.

Yes, said the old man, the child told you truth, and more would he have told you an ye would have suffered him; but ye have done a thing late that God is displeased with you, for ye have lain by your sister, and on her ye have gotten a child that shall destroy you and all the knights of your realm.

Well I wot, said the queen, I bare a child by my lord King Uther, but I wot not where he is become. Then Merlin took the king by the hand, saying, This is your mother. . . . And therewith King Arthur took his mother, Queen Igraine, in his arms and kissed her, and either wept upon other.

While searching for mention of Arthur's name, we must be careful not to be misled by the dates of certain manuscripts. The *Annales Cambriae* (*Annals of Wales*) go up as far as 950, which we may take as their date of appearance. The fact that this is over 400 years after Arthur's death should at first sight give rise to some suspicion. The reasoning is, however, faulty. For what in fact are these *Annales*? Easter is celebrated, not at a fixed date, but at a different time every year. To avoid problems, tables were kept in monasteries, in which it was possible to establish its exact date for many years to come. These Easter tables consist of two columns, of which the left-hand one always carries the list of dates. The right-hand column contains enough space to record an occasional, very important event alongside the relevant date. The entry was made quite logically at the time of the event itself. Facts thus recorded in this second column are called the Easter Annals and such are the *Annales Cambriae*. Provided one does not regard every historical record *a priori* as a fake, provided one is not prepared to dismiss all historical investigation as occult, dump it on the rubbish tip and go over to more serious business, it is reasonable to assume that the information that can be gathered from annals of that kind was recorded with care, in the presence of eternity as it were, and is therefore reliable. We read in the *Annales Cambriae*:

'518: The battle of Badon, in which Arthur wore the cross of Our Lord Jesus Christ on his shoulders for three full days, and in which the Britons were victorious.

'539: The battle of Camlan, in which Arthur and Mordred are slain: and death ruled in England and Ireland.'

What we read here, recorded at the time of the event, is enough in itself to accept Arthur as a historical character. The reference to death in England and Ireland probably relates to the yellow fever or the bubonic plague which, in the sixth century, ravaged the western world almost uninterruptedly. Interestingly, this is the first occurrence of Mordred's name in a historical document.

Not so long after the entries in the *Annales* for the years 518 and 539, and in any case before the year 600, Arthur's name is mentioned again, this time in a Welsh elegy, the *Goddodin* by Aneurin. The fleeting reference occurs in verses 1141–42. The poet is talking about a warrior who slays one enemy after another in battle. There were so many corpses, says the bard, that the ravens ate their fill, 'but the warrior was not Arthur'. A reasonable hypothesis may be that, for the poet Aneurin, Arthur himself was an esteemed leader who had died not so long ago. Apparently, he was still held in high esteem in Wales because of his courage, especially by the elderly who had not only been his contemporaries, but might even once have been his comrades-in-arms.

After these two instances that date back roughly to Arthur's own time, his name does not reappear before 829, when it crops up again in the *Historia Brittonum* (*History of the Britons*) by Nennius, a Welsh cleric from Bangor, Caernarvonshire. The author's intention is to evoke past grandeur, to bolster the Britons' self-respect and to refute the accusation that they excel only in stupidity. Despite his good intentions, Nennius makes a frightful mess of it by piling up all available material without distinction. Whatever its failings, however, the rhapsodic *Historia Brittonum* is in this context a

And as they rode, Arthur said, I
have no sword. No force, said
Merlin, hereby is a sword that
shall be yours, an I may. So they
rode till they came to a lake, the
which was a fair water and
broad, and in the midst of the
lake Arthur was ware of an arm
clothed in white samite, that held
a fair sword in that hand.

Merlin told King Arthur that he that should destroy him should be born on May-day, wherefore he sent for them all, upon pain of death; and so there were found many lords' sons, and all were sent unto the king, and so was Mordred . . .

work of vital importance.

The author was apparently driven by the feeling that it was high time everything be recorded, including the popular Arthurian tradition from his native Wales. Two intriguing stories belong to this tradition. The first concerns the Carn Cabal, a prehistoric stone pile or cairn, situated at Builth Wells. Arthur's hound, Cabal, is reputed to have left its footprint in the top stone while Arthur was hunting the mythical wild boar, Twrch Trwyth, who also appears in other Celtic stories. Also in Wales there is a barrow which people call the Licat Anir. A certain Anir is buried here and Nennius has this to say about him: 'He was the son of Arthur, the soldier, and Arthur slew him and buried him here.' Nothing is said in the legends about a legitimate son of Arthur, but we shall later hear about his bastard son, Mordred, whom we previously encountered in the *Annales Cambriae*, and who is slain by Arthur in a chivalrous fight.

More interesting still is that Nennius not only describes Arthur as 'the soldier', but also gives an account of twelve battles in which Arthur was victorious. Twelve is a nice round figure and makes you stop to think; the more so since the chronicler omits one battle, the battle of Camlann. This, however, ended not in victory for Arthur, but in defeat. All the same, Nennius seems guilty of not providing enough information, rather than of deliberate deception. Moreover, someone whose only purpose was to write a highly cosmetic apology for Arthur would most probably conceal Arthur's real or imaginary attempt on his son's life. He would also undoubtedly strive for greater accuracy in the place-names associated with his hero's immortal fame. A number of place-names related to

Arthur's victories can be located on the map: the Glen (a river in Lincolnshire or Northumberland); the Dubglas, again a watercourse, near which four battles are fought, near Linnuis (Lindsey); the forest of Celidon (upper Tweed and Clyde); the Town of the Legions (Chester or Carleon); the banks of the Tribuit (a river in the Scottish Lowlands) and finally the Mons Badonicus that Gildas would have known well. Three place-names have not yet been accurately identified: a watercourse named Bassas, a fortified position named Guinnion, probably a hill-fort, and Mount Agned.

Although it all sounds pretty vague, the list contains a few interesting details. Nennius did not just give free rein to his imagination. Moreover, where concrete facts are concerned, he seems to know just how far he can stretch his credibility. With the grand possibilities of a structure based on 12 battles at the back of his mind, he could, for instance, have come up with something better than the tedious description given four times of a battle on the banks of that same Duglas. Having seen Arthur described elsewhere as 'the soldier', the description of his military status also gives an impression of reliability: 'Arthur fought against the Saxons at the side of the British kings, but he was the *dux bellorum*' (i.e., the leader in the war). In one of the existing Nennius manuscripts, we read: . . . 'although many of them were of nobler descent than he was, he was nevertheless twelve times designated commander.'

As in the *Annales Cambriae*, the *Historia Brittonum* attributes Arthur's victories to help received from heavenly regions. At the battle of Guinnion, we learn that Arthur wore 'the effigy

The name of it, said the lady, is
Excalibur, that is as much to say
as Cut-steel.

Then Merlin lodged them in a wood among leaves beside the highway, and took off the bridles of their horses and put them to grass and laid them down to rest them till it was nigh midnight.

of the Holy Mary Eternal Virgin on his shoulders'. We also read that 'on those days the heathens were routed and suffered terrible losses, thanks to the power of Our Lord Jesus Christ and of the Holy Mary, his Virgin Mother'. The difference with the *Annales* is that they only state Arthur wore Jesus' Cross at Mons Badonicus. It looks as though Nennius probably knew this tradition but thought alterations and changes of emphasis were necessary. One of his copyists found it useful to justify this by adding: 'Arthur had gone to Jerusalem where he had had a cross made of the same dimensions as the life-giving Cross, and after it had been consecrated, he had fasted for three full days and had stood watch by it at night, praying that the wood of the Lord's cross would grant him victory over the heathens, which is what happened. He also took the effigy of the Holy Virgin with him.' The relics would naturally be small and be fixed to the body armour or used to decorate the shield or banner.

Noteworthy, therefore, is the fact that while the wood of the cross is mentioned in the *Annales Cumbriae*, the 'Holy Mary Eternal Virgin' and the 'Holy Mary, Our Lord Jesus Christ's virgin mother' are added by Nennius. You obviously can't have too much of a good thing. It is, however, proof of the reliability of the *Annales* that, at the dates 518 and 539, there is no trace of the emphasis placed on the Holy Virgin by Nennius and his copyists 400 years later. When, in 518, the battle of Mons Badonicus was recorded in the Easter Annals, Mary did not yet occupy a central position in western religious life. Not until the Council of Ephesus (531) was the dogma promulgated that Mary, as the Mother of God, should be worshipped as a virgin before,

during and after the birth. Not until the sixth century did the *Ave Maria* come into vogue. The fact that Arthur, on the basis of a slowly emerging popular tradition, may to some extent have relied on her cannot be excluded *a priori* but, at that time, the compiler of the *Annales Cambriae* did not think of mentioning it. When Nennius appears on the stage, times have changed and the new fact is mentioned. The concept of the eternal virgin is also introduced. The reason for this is the desire to fit Arthur, the *dux bellorum*, as tightly as possible into the now prevailing orthodoxy. For some reason, Nennius seems to have found this particularly important. One cannot but wonder whether the historical Arthur, just like Vortigern and many other prominent figures, may not have been a supporter of the Pelagian doctrine, so that the tenth-century historian resolved to stamp out the memory of this heresy by steadfastly associating his name with that of Mary. Since it lies within her power to conquer every heresy, this is probably a sure way of checking any suspicion of Arthur's orthodoxy.

If Arthur really was a follower of Pelagius, then this procedure would clearly point to a naïve goodwill on Nennius' part, but it would also go a long way towards explaining Gildas' stubborn silence and also our hero's standing with the hagiographers of about 1100. Moreover, it is not possible to think that every written reference to him could have been systematically deleted or, in other cases, thoroughly altered in the existing documents. Every textual reference to Arthur has since become the target of detailed scientific scrutiny, so that every mention is dismissed as a matter of course as a suspect interpolation. On the other hand, no attention is paid to the

With that Merlin was vanished, and came to King Arthur aforehand, and told him how his most enemy was taken and discomfited.

All this made Merlin by his subtle craft, and there he told the king, When I am dead these tapers shall burn no longer, and soon after the adventures of the Sangreal [Holy Grail] shall come among you and be achieved.

possibility of medieval censorship. Yet, can one imagine anything simpler than a monk-copyist disregarding, without any problem of conscience, what in his own time would be considered troublesome or improper?

In any case, we have to wait until 1125, three full centuries after Nennius, before Arthur resurfaces in a serious historical context. This is in the *Historia Regum Anglorum* (*History of the English Kings*) by William of Malmesbury. He was born around 1090 in Somerset, an area we shall soon recognize as particularly 'Arthur-sensitive'. He became a monk in Malmesbury Abbey, still famous today for its library of beautiful medieval manuscripts, and later occupied the position of librarian. William was a serious scholar with a critical frame of mind and an aversion to nonsense. One can easily assume that he possessed the necessary reliable information to be able to introduce the *dux bellorum* as follows: 'Arthur, about whom, even today, there is so much nonsense in the absurd fables of the Britons [it is also possible to read 'from Brittany']; undeniably a man, who deserves better than to figure in deceptive fabrications and should be praised in truthful accounts as someone who rallied his shaken country for a long time and roused the confused minds of his fellow countrymen to action.' Is William's distinction between 'absurd' fables', 'deceptive fabrications' and 'truthful accounts' not of vital historical importance?

To use a fashionable word, we may say that William of Malmesbury's Arthur, though not by a long way 'fashionable' in a literary sense, is granted charismatic qualities for the very first time. We now have a rough idea of the historical backdrop against which his career develops. We

also possess a number of concrete details borrowed from the *Annales Cambriae* and the *Historia Brittonum* by Nennius. The time has come for a careful attempt to piece together a more or less acceptable picture of the character. This picture is coloured in no small degree by his specified status as *dux bellorum*, i.e., as leader in the war or commander-in-chief of the army.

When Arthur was born, something like 50 to 60 years had elapsed since the Romans withdrew their troops from Britain. For four centuries before that, the country had been part of the mighty, integrated empire, a situation in no way similar to a temporary occupation such as the modern European has so often experienced in an age of mobile warfare. The Roman presence lasted long enough for the population to adapt completely and regard the *Pax Romana* as a safe situation in which to be living. In time, the Britons themselves started playing an important part in the economy. Some of them carried out military, administrative and legal functions. As the ordinary man looked on, an upper layer of middle-class and even aristocratic people emerged, who regarded themselves, without the slightest trace of doubt, as subjects of the empire. Naturally, there were the worrying raids by the Saxons and their allies, and the incursions of the looting Picts represented a real threat. But even that gave rise to a not altogether unfounded us-against-them community feeling.

There was, however, a sad spectacle in store for the Roman-British as, in 407 to 410, they watched the Romans embark – this time for good – and take their armies over to the Continent. Rome fell into the hands of the Visigoths in 410 and emperor Honorius then officially informed the Britons that they would have to fend for

Why laugh ye? said the knight. This is the cause, said Merlin: there shall never man handle this sword but the best knight of the world, and that shall be Sir Launcelot or else Galahad his son, and Launcelot with this sword shall slay the man that in the world he loved best, that shall be Sir Gawaine.

31

Yea, said King Arthur, I love Guenever the king's daughter, Leodegrance of the land of Cameliard, the which holdeth in his house the Table Round that ye told he had of my father Uther. And this damosel is the most valiant and fairest lady that I know living, or yet that ever I could find.

themselves in future. The old administrative structure held good until about 450, but crumbled visibly after that. This made the task of Vortigern and Ambrosius, who were not altogether unsuccessful in trying to uphold the safety and unity of the country under considerably increasing Germanic pressure, immeasurably more difficult. Around the time when power passed from the hands of Vortigern into those of Ambrosius, sometime between 460 and 470, a man was born whom we identify as Arthur.

As far as the possibility of piecing together the scattered elements in our possession and ordering them into a coherent *curriculum vitae* of Arthur is concerned, most authors are extremely reticent. There has, however, been one exciting attempt by the French historian, Professor Jean Markale. Based on his own insight and supported by collected material, his original scheme constitutes in some way the framework and, even more importantly, the justification for the following scenario, to which some degree of probability is attributed.

It is generally accepted that Arthur was born in Cornwall. According to tradition, this happened in the west, in the cliff-top castle of Tintagel, towering above the Atlantic Ocean. This impressive fortress was, however, only built in the twelfth century, under Norman administration, alongside a much older Celtic abbey. Today, Tintagel is very much a place of pilgrimage to which tourists flock in droves. Although Tintagel castle itself must be excluded as Arthur's place of birth, the tradition is strong enough to force serious consideration of the possibility that the *dux bellorum* first saw the light of day in a place not far from there; according to some, in nearby Bossiney.

He did not necessarily belong to the very highest circles. His military career, however, seems to indicate that he came from a British family of at least some importance. The Roman influence was still strong in families of that type. The everyday language was probably the local Celtic dialect but knowledge of Latin remained a matter of status. Now that the Roman administration was practically a thing of the past, high- or low-ranking aristocrats had taken over the task of the former bureaucracy. There is a reasonable chance that they still regarded themselves as true Romans, just as Ambrosius Aurelianus did. A mingling of native and Roman blood is also possible. They still lived in style and controlled the economy, as witness the import of pottery, wines and luxury goods from Gaul and the Mediterranean area.

Situated in the extreme southwest of Britain, Cornwall had so far not been threatened by the Saxon incursions. It had on the other hand become the refuge of thousands of miserable wretches from more easterly and northerly areas who, terrorized as they were by the murderous raids of the Germanic bands, had left all their belongings behind and, compelled by necessity, had plunged headlong into the unknown. Many of them were decent, hard-working refugees, but a lot of them were homeless beggars, deserters, thieves, plunderers and other such outlaws. No respecters of persons, they threatened the peace and safety of the population. The local system of law and order in these rural parts soon proved inadequate.

When it was decided that something must be done about this, local volunteers' militias came into being. They would first amateurishly, then more professionally, take the situation in hand

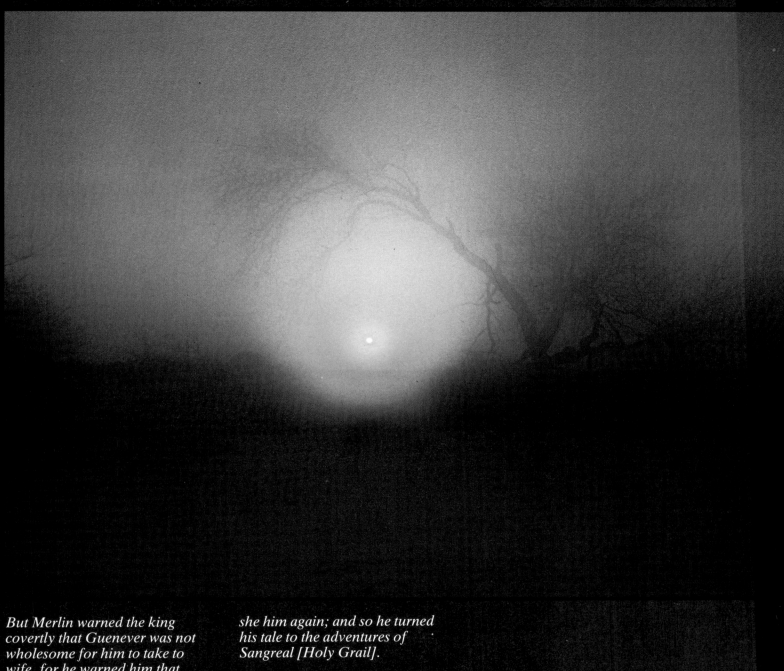

But Merlin warned the king covertly that Guenever was not wholesome for him to take to wife, for he warned him that Launcelot should love her, and she him again; and so he turned his tale to the adventures of Sangreal [Holy Grail].

But I shall send him a gift shall please him much more, for I shall give him the Table Round, the which Uther Pendragon gave me, and when it is full complete, there is an hundred knights and fifty.

and begin from then on to organize a sort of mobile police force. For a healthy and obviously ambitious young man like Arthur, it would at first be very much a sporting challenge to lead one of these armed groups, with one or two of his best friends to figure as adjutants. A nucleus was thus formed, vaguely presaging the Order of the Round Table of later literature. Characters like the famous Kay and Bedivere come to mind who, in the twelfth- and thirteenth-century epic, are described as Arthur's oldest and most faithful companions.

More and more adventurers would join the small band of men. They have to be paid, fed and housed, with the result that the simple policing initiative gets out of hand and leads to some plundering and arson. The main victims are the abbeys, in those days the economic centres, where food, well-tended livestock and considerable riches in the form of valuable cult objects are often to hand. This explains Arthur's low popularity with the contemporary clergy – the only people who kept records – and with later hagiographers.

An incidental but not altogether absurd question we can ask ourselves at this stage is whether among Arthur's trusty companions, with whom he probably shared the greatest part of the loot, there might not be a picturesque figure who, on the basis of qualities other than brute force and strength, would inspire esteem or even a certain amount of awe on the part of his leader? He might be a more intellectually gifted man, acting as organizer and counsellor, perhaps in a way even as chaplain for the few Christian soldiers who would require one. He might be a runaway monk dabbling in magic, at the same time a priest, magician, half-druid and even bard,

the possible precursor that we can imagine giving rise to the later figure of Merlin.

Seen in the context of the late fifth century, the leader and his companions would gradually constitute a real army, consisting of something like 1000 men. Arthur's fame would spread from Cornwall to Somerset, Devon, Dorset, Wales and even further. Despite Ambrosius Aurelianus' centralized authority, this is a period of anarchy, with repeated conflicts breaking out among the local tribal chiefs who, from around 440 onwards, rule over miniature kingdoms. Moreover, threatened as they are by the Picts, the Saxons and their allies, these local rulers would increasingly call on Arthur's army for help. It is hardly surprising then that Arthur, who is known for lightning-fast action, should be called upon by Ambrosius Aurelianus himself in the war against the Germans and the tribes from the north. Although many still question the accuracy of the result, nine of the battles listed by Nennius have actually been situated on the map. Even when a number of reasonable variants is taken into account, it appears that the places under consideration are scattered over Scotland, Wales and England, which seems to indicate that the mobility of Arthur's task force really was impressive. This can be attributed to nothing other than fast-moving cavalry, modelled by the *dux bellorum* on the earlier mounted cohorts of the Romans. If British horse-breeding was not up to it, it is quite possible that animals were imported from Gaul, where bigger and stronger breeds were produced. In the meantime, behind the lines, people were working hard, building up stocks of supplies, making weapons and financing the war; in short, helping to boost the moribund economy.

What tidings at Camelot? said the one. By my head, said the other, there have I been and espied the court of King Arthur, and there is such a fellowship they may never be broken, and well-nigh all the world holdeth with Arthur, for there is the flower of chivalry.

Then the king stablished all his knights, and gave them that were of lands not rich, he gave them lands, and charged them never to do outrageousity nor murder, and always to flee treason; also, by no means to be cruel, but to give mercy unto him that asketh mercy, upon pain of forfeiture of their worship and lordship of King Arthur for evermore . . .

In 518 (or thereabouts), Arthur finally reached the goal he had possibly been dreaming of all these years. The enemy was so utterly defeated at Mons Badonicus that recovery would take many decades. From then on, every time the victor appears, he is rightly regarded as the saviour of the land – a fact later echoed in the work of William of Malmesbury – and his fame with the Britons is comparable to that of, for instance, Marshal Montgomery after El Alamein. Remember that the battle of Badon is mentioned two decades later by Gildas, but with no mention of Arthur. There are several possible reasons for this, already mentioned. Gildas' silence is in fact of little importance. He does not mention Arthur but neither does he mention another general of the British army. And, however one looks at it, the fact is that there must have been such a general.

It is around this time that Ambrosius Aurelianus vanishes from the scene. Whether he dies or retires, world-weary, at Almesbury Abbey in Wiltshire, cannot be said with certainty. Now, deprived of a leader at the highest level, the local rulers soon choose Arthur, whose reputation as a strategist is enormous. There is, however, no indication that he was made king. He was therefore – a fact confirmed by Nennius – a *dux bellorum*, fighting side by side with the British kings (or tribal chiefs), although many among them were of nobler descent than he was. The title *dux bellorum* has given rise to no end of historical and philological hair-splitting, though in actual fact it clearly means nothing more than commander-in-chief. In any case, Nennius had no reason whatsoever to hush up a possible kingship. The most acceptable theory then is that

– possibly even in the time of Ambrosius – Arthur was appointed leader of a kind of confederate army. This function probably involved a number of organizational and administrative tasks, which gave him a chance to leave his stamp on the still problematical political unity. That he should thereby become much more powerful than the less important local rulers goes almost without saying. It is also possible, if the traditions from Brittany are to be believed, that he undertook campaigns in France.

Memories of the Roman period had in the meantime not died out in the world in which Arthur grew up. Stories would still circulate about a hero like Carausius, an initially mysterious figure from the Flemish marshlands where the Roman North Sea stronghold of Oudenburg was situated, who rose to the rank of admiral of the fleet and was proclaimed emperor by his British troops. This bid for the imperial title in a province of the empire which, in those days, was regarded as the end of the world, had been little more than a symbolic move. Arthur was probably too realistic to think seriously of the imperial purple in this new and thoroughly different era. He may, however, have mused on the fact that, a short while before in Gaul, Clovis had been proclaimed king (481) and been thrilled by the idea that events seemed to point to him as the successor to Ambrosius Aurelianus, generally regarded as the king of the Britons.

Both the *Historia Brittonum* and the *Annales Cambriae* belie the notion that Arthur finally adopted the title officially, which in no way means that he did not, *de facto*, become the uncrowned leader of his people.

Arthur has never completely vanished from the scene. He has lived on, in the poetic dreams of

And so on a time it happed that Merlin showed to her in a rock whereas was a great wonder, and wrought by enchantment, that went under a great stone. So by her subtle working she made Merlin to go under that stone to let her wit of the marvels there, but she wrought so there for him that he came never out for all the craft he could do. And so she departed and left Merlin.

Unto this counsel five kings assented, and so they passed forth with their host through North Wales, and came upon Arthur by night, and set upon his host as the king and his knights were in their pavilions. King Arthur was unarmed, and had laid him to rest with his Queen Guenever.

the English, until this very day. He is probably° remembered more vividly than a number of rulers whose historical authenticity is beyond °doubt. For the ordinary man or woman, he appears a genuine historical figure, just as real as William the Conqueror, King Alfred or Queen Elizabeth I.

The time did come, however, when he actually had to depart these earthly surroundings. The *Annales Cambriae* are quite clear on this account: they situate the event in 539. Between the battle of Mons Badonicus and this acceptable date for Arthur's death, we can postulate a flourishing interlude for him and his people. The Saxon threat had in a large measure been warded off; the organization of the country could once again be taken in hand and the economy restored, while the Celtic spirit seems to have reasserted itself. All this is more or less reminiscent of the fairy-tale kingdom of King Arthur as presented

by imaginative poets in the light of the high Middle Ages of around 1200.

The situation, however, did not remain as it was. Political rivalry and personal ambitions began to resurface after the relative unity against the enemy. Fighting started again, this time between the ageing Arthur and the lesser, subordinate rulers. A civil war broke out, in which he was confronted with what appears to be a formidable opponent known by the name of Medraut and, in the later documents, as Mordred. The emerging conflict is linked with Mordred's double treason. Having been appointed to rule in Arthur's absence, he had seduced Arthur's presumably younger wife – who possibly serves as a model for Guinevere – and begun the struggle against Arthur. According to a deeply rooted tradition, both were to perish in the resulting battle of Camlann. The British, even the Celtic, *Götterdämmerung* had set in for good.

*Then the king let rear and devise
in the same place whereat the
battle was done a fair abbey . . .*

3. ARTHUR'S WORLD

Then it befell that Arthur and many of his knights rode a-hunting into a great forest . . .

One enormous appeal of the Arthur figure lies in the mystery with which it is shrouded.

However vague Arthur's historical profile may be, it is nevertheless possible to find some help with which to reconstruct the world and the times in which he lived through archaeology. Even the interested tourist soon understands that the Arthurian sphere goes beyond the offices and lecture halls of historians and philologists. In place after place, he will see evidence that many a trace left by people from the Dark Ages on the landscape of Great Britain and even Brittany is directly related to it. The time has now come to consider this phenomenon.

I have hinted that Arthur's companions included a number of warriors who were to be recalled centuries later in the literature devoted to the Round Table. Archaeology enables us to mention Tristan in this context as well, because, remarkably enough, he has left an impressive archaeological trail behind him. At Fowey, close to Menabilly, on the Channel side of what, at this spot, is the narrow Cornish peninsula, and as the crow flies, some twenty miles south of Tintagel, there is a monolith alongside the road – a slightly trapezoid commemorative column from the sixth century. It is a good two metres high and bears, although very weathered and split at the top, the still visible, vertically engraved Latin inscription: '*Drustanus hic iacit cunomori filius*,' which in

English translates as: 'Drustanus, the son of Cunomorus, rests here'. Drustanus corresponds to Tristan; Cunomorus is the Latin form for the British Cynvawr. The latter was a prince who died at the beginning of the sixth century. As a contemporary of Ambrosius Aurelianus, he held sway over the old Dummonia which included Cornwall and whose power extended as far as Brittany. From the ninth century onwards, he is – just like Arthur – portrayed as a fierce enemy of the clergy by the writers of the saints' lives, which may in fact mean that he was either a Pelagian or a worshipper of the ancestral gods. The name Drustanus, or Tristan, was of Pictish origin but was also fairly common in Wales and Cornwall. It may have been that of a young warrior who was one of Arthur's officers and was later regarded as a knight of the Round Table. Only a few miles away from the Tristan stone is Castle Dore, a hill-fort where Cynvawr built his residence around 500. Wrmonoc, a monk from Landewednack in Cornwall, tells us in his *Life of St Paul* that Cynvawr was also called Mark, clearly the name of the king who, as an older man, took Isolde as a wife. This seems to indicate that in the famous legend of *Tristan and Isolde*, the old Mark need not necessarily be Tristan's uncle. Apparently Mark is originally the father whose young bride deceives him with his son but, in the famous romance, he becomes the uncle.

Now, tell me, said Arthur, how far am I from Camelot? Sir, ye are two days' journey therefrom.

This may simply be an attempt to sugar the pill of Isolde's adulterous love. However, if we read the twelfth-century text by the minstrel Béroul, it is clear that Tristan can to a certain extent also be regarded as Mark's foster-son. This is possibly related to a Celtic custom which involved putting one's children, for educational reasons, in the care of other people for a time. In this case, the experiment was not exactly successful.

Running more or less parallel to the road from Chippenham to Marlborough in Wiltshire is the Wansdyke. It is a formidable and extensive line of defence dating back to the time of Ambrosius Aurelianus, and therefore of Arthur, originally 45, and now still 12 miles long, built to protect the southwest of Britain from the possibility of a German invasion from the Thames Valley. It consists of an initially deep though now, centuries later, naturally less sharply delineated, but still broad trench, with somewhat eroded ramparts running along the north side. When the Saxons settled here later, they were so impressed by these daunting earthworks that they gave them the name of their god, Wodan. It is, unfortunately, no longer possible to say what these earthworks were originally called in the days of Arthur and his people. Moreover, it is a mystery to some authors how such an infinitely long line of defence could be manned and defended. Even when we allow for a – now missing – strong stockade constituting the upper structure and narrow, easily guarded passages at the places where present-day roads and footpaths cross the trench and ramparts, it must have been an extremely difficult task. All the same, there is no need for a wild imagination to be able to picture strategic earthworks of this kind being inspected

Anyone who walks along the Wansdyke, surrounded by the beautiful countryside of southern England, will look for the many places where the feeling of Arthur's proximity can so easily be experienced. You cannot but think of the Mons Badonicus as described by the serious scribe of the *Annales Cambriae*, by Gildas and by Nennius; it was the scene of his decisive victory which was won in the south of England. Where exactly was it that the *dux bellorum*, a relic of Jesus' cross fixed to his armour, hacked away at the Saxons, as if possessed, for three days and three nights without interruption, slaying 960 of them singlehanded?

Opinions differ on the answer to this question. Geoffrey of Monmouth does not doubt for one moment that the place is Bath, the Roman spa, the old Aqua Sulis. Another serious contender seems to me to be the Badbury Rings in Dorset, situated not far from an old military road in one of the prettiest spots along the road from Blanford to Wilborne. Badbury Rings is a fortified hill only 35 metres high, but occupying an excellent strategic position and surrounded by three lines of ramparts. Some believe these fortifications to be too far removed from what might be regarded as the front line of that time to be a possible Badon site. Surely, however, it is not out of the way to suggest that Arthur may have had to cope with a surprise offensive into which the Saxons had recklessly, with a sense of now-or-never, thrown the main body of their available troops. As in a modern *Blitzkrieg*, they had very quickly and in overwhelming numbers broken through the British lines. Anyone who remembers what happened in the Second World War can guess what followed: supply and

Then she rode into a valley where many great stones were, and when she saw she must be overtaken, she shaped herself, horse and man, by enchantment into a great marble stone.

army was cut off from its base, surrounded and utterly destroyed.

Some establish a link between Mons Badonicus and the hill-fort of Liddington castle and its surroundings. Liddington castle is situated near the road from Marlborough to Swindon, once a Roman road, and the mysterious Ridgeway. The Ridgeway, which in this area usually runs through high grounds parallel to the Wansdyke, probably came into being as early as the Old Stone Age. Part of it, now clearly defined by boards and signposts, stretches from prehistoric Avebury in Wiltshire to Ivinghoe Beacon in Herefordshire, some thirty miles to the northwest of London, which, as the crow flies, is a distance of about sixty miles. Though taken over in places by modern roads, the Ridgeway, varying in width from that of an ordinary street to a decent footpath, has by and large preserved its prehistoric or at least rural character. It is generally accepted that it was once a sort of pilgrim's way leading to the holy area of megalithic Avebury or, along a branch route, to Stonehenge.

Towards the end of the westward journey, the traveller sees a number of hill-forts sprinkled along the Ridgeway as it winds its way through the gently undulating landscape. These hill-forts show traces of having been occupied and used in Arthur's time. One of them is the previously mentioned Liddington castle, 300 metres above sea-level, a huge rectangular fortress surrounded by ramparts and with enough room inside to accommodate a strong army detachment, including cavalry. Using the Ridgeway, Arthur's army could have concentrated here. The small village of Baydon – though this is almost too good to be true – is only a small distance away from here and some five miles away from Marlborough. Marching out from Liddington castle, the advancing Britons could have annihilated the Saxon army on the hill at Baydon. After three days, the Saxons took to their heels and fled, retreating northwards in the direction of the Thames Valley. The defeated Saxons would have fled along the broad Vale of White Horse, on whose flanks many skeletons would later be turned up by the plough. These are quite possibly the mortal remains of the war casualties who died during the retreat and were hastily buried.

Anyone who practises Arthurian tourism should try not to miss the 150-metre-high iron-age fort of Brent Knoll in Somerset. It is situated at Berrow, near the Bristol Channel. The chances are that this really is the world of the legend, in which this sturdy fortress is called the Mount of Frogs. This is where Arthur and his friends ran into trouble with three giants and where Ider, the knight, lost his life. The assumption that the story is related to a strategic manoeuvre on Arthur's part should in the meantime certainly not be excluded.

Close to the border with Somerset and 6 miles north of the small town of Sherborne, there is in Dorset a hill some 170 metres high, named South Cadbury Castle. Its flanks are thickly overgrown so that the profile of a typical hill-fort surrounded by four lines of ramparts and their trenches cannot be recognized at first sight. Anyone who actually takes the trouble to climb the hill and, having reached the top, looks to the northwest, will, in reasonably good weather, see Glastonbury Tor lying 11 miles away, in fine beautiful hilly countryside. Long before our time, in 1542, the antiquarian John Leland stood here and, on coming home, noted: 'Passed the church

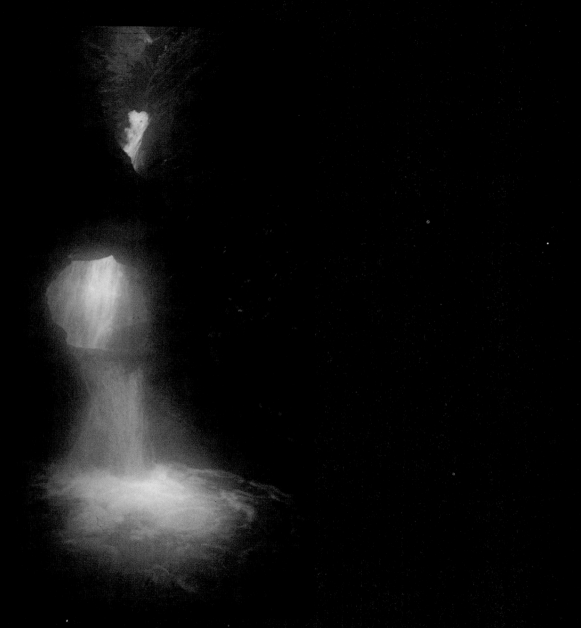

*And so they rode, and came into
a deep valley full of stones, and
thereby they saw a fair stream of
water; above thereby was the
head of the stream a fair
fountain . . .*

And so they came into a deep forest, and by fortune they were nighted, and rode long in a deep way . . .

of South Cadbury, there is Camelot, once a famous stronghold or castle, situated at the top of a great "tor" or hill and wonderfully embellished by nature. In the upper part of the elevation are trenches or ramparts crossed by a transverse earth passage. A lot of gold, silver and copper Roman coins was uncovered by the plough. The population cannot tell us anything except that they have heard that Arthur often stayed at Camelot.'

The name Camelot was not invented by Leland, but is a literary reference. It was used for the first time in the twelfth century by the French poet Chrétien de Troyes to denote Arthur's place of residence. What is remarkable is the fact that Arthurian folklore reaches a kind of critical density in the vicinity of Cadbury Castle. There is a local tradition, also known in Wales, that the hill is hollow and that Arthur and his companions sleep there. On St John's (December 27) and Christmas nights, however, they ride out on their snorting steeds, surrounded by their hounds, and make their way to the watering-place near the church of nearby Sutton Montis. Every so often, one of the horses will lose a silver shoe. The locals call the hilltop Arthur's Palace; fairies and suchlike unreal creatures live there. On the path that runs up from the village, Arthur's Well is on the left-hand side. But there is no proof whatsoever that Cadbury Castle was ever called Camelot by the people in the neighbourhood. Leland, however, was struck by the river Cam burbling only a stone's throw away, and by the fact that the villages of West Camel and Queen Camel are situated not far from here. In Ian Devries' *Keltische Religion*, there is mention of a Celtic deity called Cemenelus or Camulos. I cannot help thinking here of the Kemmelberg

near Ypres in Flanders, one of the tragic battlefields of the First World War. Need it be thought inconceivable that Camelot, i.e., Cadbury Castle, might be related to a sanctuary – of which traces have been found – dedicated to Cemenelus? And was this not the place of departure from which Arthur would later rule over the fairy-tale kingdom of medieval poetic fantasy?

The prominent Arthurian specialist Geoffrey Ashe, though he omits the Cemenelus element, in no way underestimates the possibility of a place-name link-up between Cadbury Castle and the nearby river Cam. He also mentions Camlann, where Arthur and Mordred fought their fatal battle. The location of this event is unknown. The *Annales Cambriae* provide us with no geographical location. Some have thought of the geographically unlikely Camnoglanna in Cumberland. Others opt for the meadows along the river Cam near Camelford in Cornwall, which, however, cannot be reconciled with the development of military events in Arthur's time. Close by there is an early medieval bridge called Slaughter Bridge, a name that strongly appeals to the imagination, but is probably derived from an event that took place in a ninth-century war. A late Celtic memorial stone was discovered in the vicinity of the bridge with a Latin inscription in which it was believed Arthur's name could be recognized; this turned out to be a mistake.

For all these reasons, a good candidate for the location of the battle of Camlann remains the bank of the Cam, at the foot of Cadbury Castle, a place where many convincing signs of a mass grave have been discovered in the fields. This place fits perfectly into the story. It is easy to imagine that Arthur and his followers, besieged

*And so they took their leave and
departed, and took their shipping
at Sandwich, and passed forth by
Flanders, Almaine, the
mountains, and all Italy, until
they came unto Lucius.*

And he holdeth Table Round: and in his person the most manly man that liveth, and is like to conquer all the world, for unto his courage it is too little . . .

in Cadbury Castle, were defeated while attempting a desperate sally. Understandably (according to Geoffrey Ashe), the dying Arthur would want to be taken to the nearby Glastonbury Abbey. This may have been done in secret, with important consequences for the further development of the legend.

It was not before 1966 that large-scale archaeological exploration was carried out on Cadbury Castle. The excavations conducted by Professor Leslie Alcock showed that the hill had been occupied practically without interruption since 4000 BC, so the possibility of a Cemenelus sanctuary in the old Celtic period need not necessarily be excluded. With the area known by the local inhabitants as Arthur's Palace at its centre, the upper earth layers revealed impressive fortifications and traces of a large settlement from the Arthurian period, where something like 1000 people could have lived in safety. The ground traces of a number of wooden dwellings, and the remains of strong stone defences, point to Cadbury Castle as the most imposing inhabited hill-fort of the time. If Arthur really was a historical figure, then this place stands to be regarded, on convincing archaeological grounds, as the permanent headquarters of such a prominent chief or even king and may, for the sake of convenience, be called Camelot.

What is remarkable is the fact that Arthur's world extends as far as continental Brittany. In the medieval romances, the knights of the Round Table ride from Wales to Armorica without having to cross the Channel; and we continually meet Arthurian figures in the world of Breton legends. The lake district of Paimpont (Ille-et-Vilaine) is the dwelling-place of the same fairies as those from Cornwall and Somerset; they keep their lovers captive in the nearby Forest of Brocéliande, in *Le val sans retour* (the valley of no return). This area is considered to be the county of origin of Lancelot du Lac. All of this is related to the Britons' exodus from Cornwall and Wales when, in the late sixth century, the Saxons broke through and the west was finally overrun.

And thus was the beginning of
the first journey of the Britons
and Romans, and there were
slain of the Romans more than
ten thousand, and great joy and

mirth was made that night in the
host of King Arthur.

4.   THE LITERARY HERO

Wherefore they advised them in no wise to move no more war against that noble conqueror Arthur, for his might and prowess is most to be doubted, seeing the noble kings and great multitude of knights of the Round Table, to whom none earthly prince may compare.

A historical figure, i.e., a man of flesh and blood, is doubtless what Arthur was for the ordinary man and woman who heard the stories that were told about him. It is clear that these tales were recounted by itinerant storytellers, the professional entertainers of the time, at feasts, annual fairs and near popular places of pilgrimage. The stories were thus part of a particularly effective circuit – governed by simple mathematical laws – of word-of-mouth diffusion, apparently nearly as efficient as our modern media. In the *Speculum Caritatis* by Ailred of Riévaulx, a monk from the Yorkshire abbey of the same name, the writer recounts a remarkable anecdote. Among the abbey's novices there was one who shamefully confessed that he could not bring himself to shed a single tear when reading edifying books or listening to pious sermons, although he had often wept in the past on hearing the stories 'of an unknown Arthur'.

After centuries of reliance on popular tradition, together with here and there a scanty, generally disputed snip of information in an almost inaccessible chronicle, a book written in Latin finally appeared in 1136 that apparently put an end once and for all to any uncertainty about Arthur, now plainly called King Arthur. The book is the *Historia Regum Britanniae* (*History of the Kings of Britain*) by Geoffrey of Monmouth (1100–51), a prelate who borrowed his name

from the town in South Wales where he was born. At the time of his birth, half a century had elapsed since William the Conqueror had become the master of what from then on would be called England. A new Anglo-Norman nobility and clergy had risen from William's circle of protégés. As newcomers in the land of which they had suddenly become the masters, they seemed curious to know about the past of what for them was a largely unknown world. A need for information arose, to be answered by Geoffrey of Monmouth, a Welshman, possibly with Breton blood in his veins. As a result, his *Historia* became what amounted to a bestseller.

Geoffrey attributes the foundation of the British Kingdom to a descendant of Aeneas named Brutus who, after the Trojan War, had conquered the island of Albion. The book ends with the Saxon invasion and the downfall of the Britons. Something like a third of the book is devoted to Arthur and his time. For the first time, Arthur appears as a feudal prince with all the trappings. His origins, his court, his family relations, his rise to fame, his impressive feats of war and, finally, his fatal defeat are described in great detail. This all takes place in a world that is a faithful reflection of twelfth-century knighthood, with no insight at all into the Dark Ages and their own specific atmosphere.

In no way did this devalue the work in the eyes

And then the senators made
ready for his enthronization.
And at the day appointed, as the
romance telleth, he came into
Rome, and was crowned
emperor by the pope's hand, with
all the royalty that could be
made, and sojourned there a
time, and established all his lands
from Rome into France . . .

So they mounted on their horses, armed at all rights, and rode into a deep forest and so into a deep plain. And then the weather was hot about noon, and Sir Launcelot had great lust to sleep.

of the writer's contemporaries. They seemed perfectly happy with their fat, easily readable *Historia Regum Britanniae*. The enthralling Geoffrey is unmistakably a born raconteur, but that is precisely the snag: as a storywriter he writes epic fiction that has little to do with history. By analogy with Herodotus, he is sometimes called 'the father of all lies'. Meanwhile, we should not lose sight of the fact that we are indebted to the notoriously unreliable Greek historian for a sizeable share of our knowledge of the ancient world. As far as Monmouth is concerned, the question has recently arisen as to whether his *Historia* might not also contain nuggets of truth from the oral tradition and lost documents. Be that as it may, it is clear that Geoffrey played fast and loose with the facts. His story of Arthur's conquest of Ireland, Norway and Gaul, in no way supported by historical evidence, is the chief proof of this.

As far as Arthur's campaigns in Gaul are concerned, a number of new and highly astonishing facts have recently been brought to light by Geoffrey Ashe. This obstinate English researcher has studied the fifth-century wars between the Romans and the Visigoths in what is now France, although he is well aware of a number of problems related to currently accepted chronology, which he has yet to scrutinize more closely. His tentative conclusion is that the Romans almost certainly called on the overseas Britons – until now mistaken for the continental Bretons – for help. Moreover he has found traces of a mysterious British army leader. In the *History of the Goths* (551) by Jordanes, and in chronicles derived from this, the mysterious figure is called Riotmus or Riothamus. In Breton texts, however, he is identified by the chronicle

writers as Arthur. This could mean that Riothamus was a military or political title, or it could have been a second name for Arthur.

However little we may trust Geoffrey's book, we shall have to refer repeatedly, since there is no way round it, to his *Historia Regum Britanniae*. Ashe's research has shown that not only did Geoffrey use the *Annales Cambriae*, Nennius and Gildas, but that he apparently relied on other sources as well, possibly rather more literary. Before 1100 an anonymous Welsh author had already written down the much older traditional *Culhwch and Olwen*, in which Arthur appears as a protagonist and as a sovereign ruler whose faithful companions already include Kay and Bedivere. This story seems to have provided Geoffrey with the basis for Arthur's imaginary expedition to Ireland at the head of an army consisting of Britons, Frenchmen and Normans.

The *Historia Regum Britanniae* was soon imitated, with new material occasionally being added to the story. Nobody at the time seems to have taken exception to the fact that the French *Roman de Brut* (1155) by the Jersey-born Robert Wace, which was written for Queen Eleanor of Aquitaine, is little more than an adaptation of Geoffrey's book. Robert Wace was in fact the first author to mention the Round Table and its knights, a fact which may point to an existing oral tradition and which was to determine the further development of the Arthurian material.

There is a story in the South Cadbury area that Arthur lies asleep in a cave under the hill that rises above the village. Stories of that kind also circulate elsewhere in England, Wales and Scotland. This tradition matches the unconscious primeval archetype of the slain hero. It is expected that he will one day rise, achieve the

When Arthur held his Round
Table most plenour, it fortuned
that he commanded that the high

which in those days was called
Kynke Kenadonne, upon the
sands that marched nigh Wales.

And there were all the knights of the Round Table only those that were prisoners or slain at a recounter. Then at the high feast evermore they should be fulfilled the whole number of an hundred and fifty, for then was the Round Table fully complished.

ideals that remained unattainable during his lifetime and reign once more over his people in a Golden Age. Archetypes of that kind are psychological representations, patterns of thought or expectation, that play an important part in the depth psychology of Carl-Gustav Jung, Sigmund Freud's contemporary. They crystallize out, as it were, from the myth-laden, age-old experiences of mankind; they are contained, as potential experience patterns, in the deepest so-called collective unconscious and may suddenly resurface in response to particular circumstances. As far as Arthur – himself a more or less historical rationalization of much older archetypal contents – is concerned, this resurfacing process appears to take place on a large scale from the twelfth century onwards. A new literature is born, that in no time at all gives new life to him and his companions.

The causes of this are to be sought in both political and cultural circumstances. In 1154, Henry II, the son of Geoffrey Plantagenet, ascended the throne of England, which he was to occupy until his death in 1189. Married to Eleanor of Aquitaine two years before, he included in his kingdom not only England, but all of the western half of France as well, containing Anjou, which gave its name to the Angevin dynasty. He was without any doubt the most powerful monarch in the western world of that time. Yet his accession to the throne had been preceded by dramatic dynastic conflicts. As a result, anything that could possibly reinforce his royal authority was looked upon with a favourable eye. As an educated man (a pupil of Thomas Becket, 1117–70), he apparently realized the political advantages that could be drawn from a literature centred round an ideal

'English' kind such as Arthur, with whom he could be identified. There is a strong likelihood, however, that Queen Eleanor played a more important part in this respect.

Born in 1122, she was the grand-daughter of William IX of Aquitaine, a very picturesque and complex figure. He had participated in the first Crusade at the side of Godfrey of Bouillon. The pious nature of the expedition did not prevent him from being a notorious womanizer, which resulted in his being excommunicated by the Pope – an event that apparently did not cause him much heartbreak. It was said of him that he had a church built at his own expense, and set up a brothel with prostitutes disguised as nuns, on the same day that he opened the house of God to the public. Despite this evidence of poor taste, he was the first major southern French troubadour, writing songs that were both audacious and brilliant, sometimes even moving. His grand-daughter Eleanor probably inherited her unconventional character and enthusiasm for poetry from him. Many poets enjoyed her support and were inspired by her. As appears from his work, it is quite possible that the troubadour Bernard de Ventadour (her court poet for a time) was very much in love with her; the feeling was probably not mutual, but may have provoked the king's displeasure all the same.

At this time it was in the abbeys and cloisters that it was possible to enjoy the luxury of spiritual culture. In the castles of the nobility, a sterner atmosphere of administration, diplomacy and military preparedness prevailed. An itinerant storyteller or singer, however, was a welcome figure, especially for the noble ladies who, in this harsh world of soldiers, could find life immeasurably boring. Some minstrels succeeded

Then Sir Beaumains put on his helm anon, and buckled his shield, and took his horse, and rode after him all that ever he ~~might ride through marshes and~~ fields, and great dales, that many times his horse and he plunged over the head in deep mires, for he knew not the way, but took the ~~gainest way in that woodness~~ that many times he was like to perish.

The King and the Queen made their pavilions and their tents in that forest beside a river, and there was daily hunting and jousting . . .

in securing a position for themselves, even at courts of unimportant princes. In 1170, the singer Walter de Clusa, possibly a Fleming whose repertoire probably included a low German *Merlin* and a *Tristan*, appears as a member of the entourage of Arnold II, count of the then Flemish Guines (Pas de Calais). In France and in England, this soon became a norm, with the beautiful, dynamic Eleanor setting the example. After a stay in England and as a result of the soured relationship with her unfaithful husband, who was her junior by 11 years, the lively queen took up residence, from 1170 onwards, in Poitiers, where her glittering court was enhanced by the presence of artists, scholars and poets.

Nowhere is it clearly stated who in fact belonged to Eleanor's entourage or, later, to that of her equally artistic daughter Marie de Champagne. On the other side of the Channel, Eleanor would of course have met Walter Map, who will be mentioned again later. He was Henry II's chaplain and a satirist in Latin, the author of a series of gossipy but moral and historically remarkable sketches, entitled *De Nugis Curialium* (*The Trifles of the Court*). The court may also have included Béroul and Thomas the Englishman who, with an interval of a few decades, both composed a *Tristan* – an apparently popular subject. Obviously at very different moments in time, there is no doubt that Robert Wace, Bernard de Ventadour and Chrétien de Troyes were to be found in the proximity of either the mother or the daughter. This is perhaps also true of a certain Guyod from Provence. Under the further influence of the troubadours of Aquitaine and Provence, a world grew up where courtly love, the *fin amor* – the principles of which were laid down by André le

Chapelain, the court chaplain of Countess Marie, in his *De Arte Honeste Amandi* – was the subject of conversations, parlour games and poetry. Entirely new forms of social intercourse came into being in this somewhat frivolous atmosphere and women achieved consideration as never before.

The image of this period is largely dominated by Chrétien de Troyes. Born in 1130, he was possibly a landless nobleman or, according to some, a cleric from Champagne. From 1160 onwards, he wrote a number of Arthurian romances, including *Erec*, *Cligès*, *Lancelot*, *Yvain* and *Perceval* (1182), a work which at his death remained unfinished. All these refined, often intricate romances, as were those which were written in imitation of Chrétien's work, bear witness to the enormous popularity of the Arthurian material in the second half of the twelfth century. It was a period in which writing meant writing about Arthur, the Round Table and everything that could be associated with it. It should be stressed here that this all happened on French soil and in French, although the phenomenon extended almost immediately to the neighbouring countries, but with the French texts as models. How did such a fashion, which constituted the high point of medieval literature in western Europe, take root? Why should the literature of the Continent, in particular that of France and Norman, and therefore still French-speaking, England, be suddenly dominated by what is an explicitly British subject?

One of the poets who completed Chrétien's unfinished *Perceval* refers in his story to a certain Blihis, whose stories about Gawain had been particularly popular with the count of Poitiers, the father, *nota bene*, of Queen Eleanor. Blihis

Her name was Annowre, and this lady came to King Arthur at Cardiff; and she by fair promise and fair behests made King Arthur to ride with her into that Forest Perilous; and she was a great sorceress; and many days she had loved King Arthur . . .

And as they rode through that forest they came by a fair well where Sir Tristram was wont to be . . .

then appears in the rapid succession of new Arthur stories under easily recognizable variants such as Bledhri, Bleheri(s), Bliobeheri(s), Blihis and even Blaise. Surprisingly enough, it seems that Blihis was probably not an imaginary character but a historical figure. In 1194, the Welsh cleric Giraldus Cambriensis (1145–1223), in his *Description of Wales*, mentions a certain Bledri, a famous storyteller, who lived shortly before his own time. Unfortunately, Giraldus restricts himself to a mere mention of the name. Reliable Welsh archives also point to a certain Bledri whose father's name was Cadivor, a nobleman and big landowner who collaborated with the Norman authorities. What is striking is the fact that the grave of Gawain, about whom Blihis or Bledri told such exciting stories to the duke of Poitiers, is thought to be situated at Ross (Pembrokeshire) in Wales – a remarkable link if ever there was one. Bledri appears in several official documents as *Latinarius*, which in the context means translator. This proves that he acted as link-man and Welsh-French interpreter for the Norman authorities. At the death of his father, Bledri inherited the small village of Manorbeer, the birthplace of Giraldus Cambriensis who in turn was outspokenly in favour of co-operation with the Angevin dynasty.

Whether this was a case of opportunism or straightforward *Realpolitik*, the fact is that the apparently polyglot Bleris – who would have known Welsh, French, Latin and Old English – seems to have made full use of the structure of the Anglo-Norman kingdom to cross over to the Continent. Taking his background into account, his was probably not the decision of a destitude adventurer. There may also have been a diplomatic or political mission; unless it was

simply a matter of a rich man's son and educated Welshman wanting to get acquainted with a different, cultural and artistic, world. In any case, he had means enough – especially in his head, with his apparently unrivalled ability as a storyteller. Thomas the Englishman, who composed an early *Tristan*, was to say of him that 'he knew the history of all the counts and all the kings of Britain'. An anonymous writer later added: 'Bleris knew all the stories about the Grail' – an important remark.

As an example of the way in which the Arthur theme reaches the Continent, the Bleris case is most convincing; this is also borne out by the fact that he eventually appears as one of the characters in the later romances. It was probably quite common for adventurous vagrants from Wales and Cornwall who had natural abilities as storytellers, singers and actors, to travel to western France, which now belonged to their own king, and present what to the continental nobility was an exotically sounding repertoire. The French minstrels were simultaneously being attracted by the Norman nobility in England, so that a fruitful exchange arose between the two regions. Clearly, this osmosis was already taking place at a very early stage. It is enough here to recall the Bodmin incident in 1113 as reported by Herman of Tournai, between the visitors from Laon and the local population. Fifty years after the battle of Hastings (1066) and over 20 years before the appearance of Geoffrey of Monmouth's successful book, Arthur was by no means unknown to these clerics. The Plantagenet kingdom extended to both sides of the Channel, so it is clear that popular stories about Arthur, rounded off and stylized by professional entertainers, could easily be found in France, all

My fellows, said King Arthur, look that ye be of good cheer, for to-morn I will be in the field with you and revenge you of your enemies. So that night King

Arthur and his knights reposed themself.

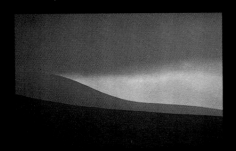

Ye say well, said Sir Tristram, now I assign you to meet me in the meadow by the river of Camelot, where Merlin set the peron.

the more since Breton *conteurs*, whose cultural heritage also included these stories, were almost certainly involved. Furthermore, if the influence of Geoffrey's authoritative, albeit unreliable *Historia* is taken into account, the sudden popular appeal of King Arthur on the Continent need not at all be considered a mystery.

What is mysterious is above all the unexpected emergence of a number of apparently new details, all related to a mysterious object which Bleris seems to have known about: the so-called Grail, which first appears with Chrétien de Troyes.

It was probably in the year 1200 that Robert de Boron finished writing a book that, unfortunately, he never really completed. It should originally have consisted of three parts: *Joseph d'Arimathie*, *Merlin* and *Perceval*. The textbooks usually consider half the trilogy as lost, but even the Flemish poet Jacob van Maerlant (1235–92), when he wrote his *Merlijns Boec* (1260), clearly in imitation of Boron, had to manage with no more than what we know of the work, which tends to indicate that the French writer probably never completed his story. The writers who completed Chrétien's *Perceval*, however, repeatedly referred to it. Filled out with other material, Boron's *Roman de l'Estorie dou Graal*, as the unfinished trilogy is thought to have been called, was turned by an anonymous author into a new whole, known as the prose *Lancelot* or the vulgate *Lancelot*. This was a most impressive compilation of all the then known traditions. Walter Map, whose name has already been mentioned, is repeatedly and emphatically referred to in the manuscripts as the author. This finds no favour in the eyes of the scholars. On the basis of the date of Map's death (1209), objections are raised of a chronological nature, to

which the argument is added that this courtier and apparently very mundane cleric could not possibly have found the time to write such an extensive work. The latter especially appears to be a fairly weak, scholastic argument. I may be able to provide another. The explicit theological nature of the vulgate *Lancelot* offers no psychological similarity with the waggish and impressionistic nature of Map's *De Nugis Curialium*. I shall have to reconcile myself to the idea that the vulgate *Lancelot* was the work of a group of laymen or monks from a Cistercian abbey in Champagne, where it may have originated in the period 1215–30.

More important than wondering how Master Map spent his spare time is the appearance between 1200 and 1216 of *Parzival*, by the German minstrel Wolfram von Eschenbach. Though he imitates Chrétien de Troyes, Wolfram is in many ways at odds with the Frenchman who may not have done justice to history. This is in any case what he emphatically says, adding just as emphatically and repeatedly that he has received important additional information from a certain 'Meister Kyot, der Provenzal'. Whoever he may have been, this unknown Kyot could have been called nothing but Guyod in his own language. He is the Guyod whose possible presence in the entourage of Marie de Champagne has already been mentioned. Whether Wolfram himself was ever one of the many poets who basked in Marie's reflected glory and whether that was how he met a certain Guyod from Provence is probably much too bold a question. What is sure is that he had a certain knowledge of French, or he could not have been inspired by Chrétien de Troyes. Where then did he acquire his – possibly passive – knowledge of French?

*prophesied that in that same
place should fight two the best
knights that ever were in Arthur's
days, and the best lovers.*

5. MEDIEVAL BESTSELLERS

And then were they ware of a castle that was fair and rich, and also passing strong as any was within this realm.

It would be very difficult to overlook the fact that these works, together with many others that have not been mentioned, look singularly alike. In particular, I am thinking here of the story itself: not the stylistic, poetic or, at this stage at least, not the hidden mythical or mystical aspects of the works. Yet there are considerable differences and blatant contradictions in the contents, too. The result is that, as far as the epic subject matter is concerned, the reader rapidly gets the impression of a confused muddle, often devoid of any logical structure. Nevertheless, I now propose to give a general, though incomplete and obviously vague, idea of what these sometimes incredibly complicated romances are all about.

The central figure is Arthur, represented as a typical Christian prince of the feudal period. His father is Uther Pendragon – which means Dragon's Head – king of the Britons, who dies shortly after the birth of his son. The new-born child is entrusted to the care of a magician, Merlin, who looks after his upbringing and leaves him for a time with the knight Ector. When the youngster is 15, Merlin thinks it is time to put an end to the country's state of political confusion caused by Uther's death. He convenes the nobility in London. Arthur manages to remove a sword from a block of marble in which it is embedded. According to an inscription on the weapon itself, this feat proves that he is the lawful king of England, also called Logres. The young ruler will nevertheless repeatedly need to defend his right to the throne by force of arms. In Tintagel castle, where he was born, he marries Guinevere, the daughter of the king of Cornwall and the most beautiful woman in Britain.

Arthur's splendid sword soon breaks, but he receives a new one, called Excalibur, from the hands of the Lady of the Lake. She is a mysterious creature, probably a fairy, who has desires on Merlin whom she will later seduce. She plays a considerable, sometimes decisive role in the story, all the more so because she brought up Sir Lancelot. There is also Morgan; she too stands with one foot in reality and the other in the world of fairies. This fearful magician is the daughter of Igraine, Arthur's mother, and her first husband Gorlois, which makes her the king's stepsister. In many texts she appears to hate his knights and even to have sworn to bring about their destruction, while she never misses an opportunity of denting their pride, obviously irritated by the stubbornness and lack of humour which indeed characterize the heroes of these stories. Unaware of the blood-relationship, Arthur, whose fidelity in marriage seems somewhat shaky, gets Morgan with child. The child is christened Mordred and it is he – both Arthur's son and nephew – who, at the end of the story, will cause Arthur's downfall and that of his

*And then will he come and set
wild-fire on every part of the
castle, and I shall get you out at a
privy postern, and there shall ye
have your horse and your
harness.*

There was cried by the coasts of Cornwall a great tournament and jousts, and all was done by Sir Galahalt the haut prince and King Bagdemagus, to the intent to slay Launcelot . . .

knights. On that occasion, Arthur has Bedivere return his sword Excalibur to the Lady of the Lake. Various places are named where this might have occurred: the bridge of Pomparles, in actual fact le Pont Périlleux, the Dangerous Bridge, in Glastonbury, Somerset, as well as two lakes in Cornwall, Loe Pool and more particularly the eerie Dozmary Pool in the lonely surroundings of Bodmin Moor.

The importance of Merlin in these romances – in which many consider him to be the most enigmatic and attractive character – has already become apparent. He appears ubiquitously as Arthur's counsellor and prime minister, invested with a considerable, though not precisely specified authority. The figure was probably inspired by the legendary sixth-century Welsh bard Myrddin, which – bearing in mind the prominent position of such outspoken poets at the court – would explain his great influence on the monarch and his entourage. This *éminence grise* is first encountered in Geoffrey of Monmouth's *Historia*, in which he figures as a counsellor for Ambrosius Aurelianus and Vortigern before Arthur even appears. His supernatural gifts enable him to arrange for Uther Pendragon to sleep with Igraine and get her with child. Thanks to his tremendous knowledge of the occult, he has long since prepared for Arthur's arrival and has minutely set the stage for his entrance into the world, whereupon he will guide and protect him continuously, much like a director of dramatic events.

Merlin is a protean figure, endowed with superhuman wisdom and great occult powers – which today we would call parapsychological. As a magician, he is by no means a self-made man.

To use once again a modern expression, it might be said that he is genetically fitted to fulfil his task as a magician, since he stems directly from the time that the devil decided to deliver mankind into the hands of the Antichrist. A demonic spirit in the shape of an incubus had therefore been sent to visit a young, obviously virgin nun. The nun became pregnant. Though she herself was not to blame, this created enormous difficulties. Beelzebub and his acolytes, however, seem to have been ignorant of Mendel's laws of heredity and of the hidden surprises that genes and chromosomes can spring on us. This time, the devils do not quite get what they bargained for. The child seems to have enormous magical gifts, which enable him, while he is little more than a baby, to clear his mother from blame. In perfect accordance with the uncertainties of genetics, his strange powers are dominated by the positive element which represents the psychic inheritance from his mother.

Having been vainly destined to play the role of Antichrist, Merlin, as a result, enters life as a white magician. At the centre of mysterious powers under his control and endowed with clairvoyance – a power which is shared by the druids – he becomes a great astrologer with power to read the present and the past, giving him the necessary wisdom to guide Arthur and his paladins through all imaginable difficulties. In contrast to his belligerent friends, he has an undeniable sense of what sometimes resembles black humour. Jokes and mystifications are no strangers to him and he is familiar with every trick of magic. He can take the most divergent shapes or suddenly materialize out of nothing. Neither does he shrink from tasks which apparently have more to do with engineering

Then La Beale Isoud and Sir
Tristram took their vessel, and
came by water into this land.

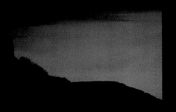

And so Sir Launcelot brought Sir Tristram and La Beale Isoud unto Joyous Gard, that was his own castle, that he had won with his own hands.

than tricks of magic. Furthermore, he is unmistakably an intellectual who, according to Robert de Boron, even keeps a secretary to whom he dictates the story of his origins and youth, as well as a lot of essential details for the Arthurian material. This secretary is called Blaise, after the French fashion, and is none other than Bleris, our old acquaintance who knows so many ancient stories.

One of Merlin's most important contributions to our story is that he suggests the idea to Arthur of the Round Table as the central point, or *omphalos*, of his kingdom. According to one version, this is a splendid piece of furniture – Guinevere's wedding present from her father. A copy of it, made at the request of Edward III around 1340, can be admired in Winchester's Guild Hall in Hampshire. Others claim that the Round Table had already been in the possession of Uther Pendragon, designed by Merlin and made by a Cornish carpenter under the magician's supervision. It is round this table, whose shape makes them all equals, that Arthur sits with the knights who arrive at the court in steadily increasing numbers. Wonderful banquets are given, during which the companions, who rapidly form a select, somewhat closed and inflexible group, speak highly of their heroic deeds. New missions are inspired by Arthur and Guinevere to whom the knights also submit their problems. The Round Table becomes the central point from which they, separately or in groups, ride out in quest of adventure and to which they return to give colourful accounts of their remarkable experiences.

Arthur and Guinevere usually reside in Camelot castle but also spend time in Caerleon in Monmouthshire, Tintagel or Winchester. Seldom

now do they envisage serious military campaigns against the Saxons and their allies. The companions of the Round Table have mainly become knights errant, a phenomenon which, under the influence of the Crusades, seems also to have occurred in reality. They imagine that they are defending the interests of their king and, through their heroic deeds, that they are bringing more glory to his name. The truth however is that they are wilful, highly self-centred individualists, with almost no other interest than their own personal reputation and destiny. Theoretically, their sights are set on the ideals of knighthood: to protect the faith, the weak, the widows and the orphans, and to maintain law and order, which – much as in a Western – they sometimes take into their own hands. They do not always distinguish between friend and foe and sometimes realize at the last moment that they are about to cut a comrade to pieces. They legalize their heroic deeds, which sometimes seem true and sometimes dubious, by promptly sending the prisoners-of-war or lonely maidens to the king, thus increasing the population of Camelot.

They are continually being called upon to rescue threatened or abducted young maidens from the claws of their tormentors, for which they are rewarded *in natura* during many a pastoral interlude. Many of their heroic deeds are inspired by the desire to please the loved one they have left behind. In pursuing this desire, they will not hesitate to look death in the eye. They prefer a fatal issue to the risk of bringing discredit on their manly honour and, as a result, of being considered unworthy by their beloved. If, on occasion, a head has to roll – which not infrequently happens – then it is hung from the saddle, according to ancient Celtic custom, and

So thus they rode until that they came to Humber bank, where they heard a cry and a doleful noise. Then were they ware in the wind where came a rich vessel hilled over with red silk, and the vessel landed fast by them.

And then they dressed their shields, and pulled out their swords, and lashed together many sad strokes as men of might; and this fighting was more than an hour, but at the last Sir Palomides waxed big and better winded, so that then he smote that knight such a stroke that he made him to kneel upon his knees.

given to the loved one as proof of bravery.

No one knows better than they what it means to lead a dangerous life. Unless they have to take them by force of arms, they knock at the doors of strange castles, often situated near water or on a precipitous cliff, which sometimes involves crossing bridges no wider than the cutting-edge of a sword. Inside, their arrival is awaited by fairies who may be attractive but not always harmless; they must play chess against invisible opponents or, more often still, are confronted with blood-curdling abominations and locked up in sinister dungeons. Having escaped from such dangers, they travel on through enchanted, frightful forests, where magicians dwell, who could very well be the descendants of the druids. They may finally arrive at a chapel where a dead man is waiting for them or where horrible ghostly apparitions and other gruesome creatures make their blood run cold; there may be a nearby churchyard where 3000 of their colleagues, murdered on the spot for unknown reasons, lie buried. They may think themselves lucky if they do not encounter spell-casting lascivious nymphs – water nymphs or others – who, through cunning magical practice, enslave them in some forest of Brocéliande from which there is no return. Through mysterious islands and attractive pleasure gardens, their route finally takes them back to Camelot, where Arthur and Guinevere are waiting impatiently to hear their stories. When boredom threatens, there is no tournament in which they cannot take part. The knights are then followed in admiration by the apparently cool, but in actual fact impatient gaze of the coquettish beauties who have taken their places in the stands. The latter do not hesitate, as in the case of Lancelot, to put their champion's devotion to the test by imposing almost unbearable humiliations.

All these incorrigible diehards often give the impression of being bloodthirsty tyrants with very little grey matter under their helmets; they seem products of the unbridled imagination of mad minstrels and frustrated clerics, and often confuse nonsense with subtlety. In their own way, however, they try to be men of goodwill, stay true to their friends and keep their word, which, in principle at least, corresponds to the ethical ideals of the then upper 10% to whom this type of literature is addressed. They obviously think that they are making the world a better place, among other things by continually putting their lives into the hands of God, like pilgrims to the Absolute, wandering through hallucinatory regions that lie outside our Euclidean three-dimensional world.

The pious hermits, who are often met along the way, seem to embody a reminiscence of the Celtic anchorites who, long ago, tried to find in solitude a way to reach the state of grace. Such encounters and conversations give rise to pious meditations that come as a surprise in this world of gaily coloured stereotypes. Furthermore, they often show signs of a moving sensitivity, as with Perceval whose very soul is moved by the sight of three drops of blood standing out very clearly in the snow. He is suddenly reminded of the beloved Blanchefleur and goes into a trance, which for more than a day makes him oblivious of the facts of reality. In Wolfram von Eschenbach, he undergoes the existential experience of compassion, in order to become a wise human being. When, like Lancelot for Guinevere, they experience a feeling of love – the courtly love from the world of Queen Eleanor and Countess Marie – it all seems strikingly genuine, as though nothing could ever thwart it.

I may never believe, said Palomides, that King Arthur will ride so privily as a poor errant knight.

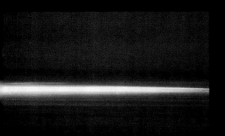

6. THE APPEARANCE OF THE GRAIL

So came in a damosel passing
fair and young, and she bare a
vessel of gold betwixt her hands;
and thereto the King kneeled
devoutly, and said his prayers,
and so did all that were there.

After Chrétien's *Perceval*, a number of new elements appear in several of the Arthur romances. These elements add an extra mysterious dimension to give these often incredible-sounding tales a disorienting force, which undeniably seems to lend a deeper meaning to what are originally the somewhat gratuitous adventures of Arthur and his companions. As far as the supernatural element is concerned, sensitive researchers take into account the possibility that such apparently new information may not be a late-medieval embelishment, but relics of a much older tradition whose meaning was in the course of time lost. Although the poets of around 1200 and later hardly know what to make of these, they use them, as well or as badly as they can, as if compelled to do so by some tangible radioactive force, but often find themselves groping in the dark. The new elements include a number of mysterious objects that seem exceptionally important for an apparently completely new character in the works concerned. Character and objects gradually grow into a logically delineated whole. This originally confusing configuration is first encountered in Chrétien de Troye's *Perceval*.

The young Perceval is brought up in the forest by his noble widowed mother, far from the dangerous world of wars and knightly violence.

The unsuspecting young man nevertheless decides to travel to Arthur's court. The moment he arrives, he sees an unknown Red Knight storm into the palace and deeply offend Queen Guinevere. Perceval rides after the culprit and slays him before pursuing his journey. One day he reaches a river and discovers a crippled, apparently even partly paralysed, nobleman, fishing from a little-boat. The man offers him hospitality in his castle and tells him not to wait for him, but to ride there immediately.

As soon as Perceval has been let into the splendid castle, he realizes that his ailing host has already arrived. A strange procession soon appears, bathed in a supernatural light. First comes a squire bearing a sword – a gift from his host. Then follows a young man with a white lance dripping blood. Bearing candle-holders with burning candles, two young noblemen precede a young maiden who is holding a vessel adorned with precious stones and radiating a blinding light. The vessel that this young maiden is carrying is described without further explanation as a 'Grail' by the poet. Finally, a second maiden arrives holding a shallow silver dish. Perceval is unable to understand what all this means and, bearing in mind the advice given to him, always to remain discreet, he dares not ask questions. The next day, on awakening, it seems as though all the inhabitants of the castle

This castle may be named the Castle Adventurous, for here be many strange adventures.

And right so he saw come in a light, that he might well see a spear great and long that came straight upon him pointling, and to Sir Bors seemed that the head of the spear brent like a taper.

have disappeared, but his horse is saddled up and waiting for him. As he is crossing the drawbridge, it is suddenly pulled up, but his mount makes a desperate leap and Perceval lands unharmed on the other side of the moat.

I shall not describe Perceval's further adventures as a wandering knight. The main thing for the moment is that, at short or long intervals, he meets up with a number of sometimes strange characters. From these he gradually learns that he has committed a grave mistake in the castle of the ailing Fisher-King, as his host appears to be called, in not asking about the meaning of the – still not further specified – Grail and bleeding lance. He finally realizes that the unspoken questions would in some way or another have cured the ailing king and put an end to the disasters and barrenness which seem to be plaguing his kingdom. His neglect now appears to be the reason for the king's enduring illness, for the unending devastation of the land and for the many deaths that are still to come. Perceval is deeply moved by this realization and swears from then on never to spend more than one single night at the same place until he has found the castle, which has apparently vanished without trace, and understood the meaning of the Grail and the lance. Just as the ensuing five-year expedition finally appears to be drawing to a close and the expectation seems founded that he will soon reach the castle, the poet suddenly switches over to another wandering knight-figure, namely Gawain, whose colourful adventures will for the time being have nothing to do with the Grail.

It is generally accepted that Chrétien's death occurred after verse 9234. As a result, nothing further is said about the Grail, the lance and the ailing Fisher-King, which could certainly not have been Chrétien's intention. Other authors later completed *Perceval*: one anonymous author, a poet who was first thought to be one Wauchier de Denain and later, because of the apparent uncertainty, was called the pseudo-Wauchier; one Manessier and one Gerbert de Montreuil. The fact is that they went on, with considerably less talent, endlessly spinning out a story which was already very much advanced; so far advanced in fact for us to believe that the end was already in sight at the time of Chrétien's death. It had probably been his intention to pick up the threads after the relation of Gawain's adventures and to guide Perceval finally to the castle of the Grail, where the knight would have delivered the Fisher-King from his misery and freed the blighted land from its barrenness and its plagues by asking about the Grail and the lance.

To discard the possibility of Chrétien's untimely death, as is sometimes done, and claim that he simply no longer believed in his plot, is an alternative that need not be taken into account. It shows a schoolmaster's mentality that lacks every understanding for the way in which the creative process develops. The author of *Perceval* probably died in 1182 or shortly afterwards; the importance of this event will, in fact, appear clearly later on.

Before we started looking at *Perceval*, it was possible, without bending the truth, to present the Arthur story as a kind of adventure novel with the occasional moving tone or exciting psychological accent, mainly due to the element of courtly love. With Chrétien, we find ourselves confronted with a number of totally unexpected elements that, in his last work, create a highly

And then Sir Bors laid him down to rest, and then he heard and felt much noise in that chamber; and then Sir Bors espied that there came in, he wist not whether at the doors nor windows, shot of arrows and of quarrels so thick that he marvelled, and many fell upon him and hurt him in the bare places.

Anon withal there came an old man into the hall, and he sat him down in a fair chair, and there seemed to be two adders about his neck; and then the old man had an harp, and there he sang an old song how Joseph of Armathie came into this land.

poetic and mysterious, even mystical, atmosphere. In a fairy-tale castle, which apparently belongs to another dimension, the hero encounters a doomed king. The handicapped, suffering king possesses a number of valuable, apparently magical objects. They can, however, be of no possible use to him unless an innocent, 'pure' knight, sent to him by fate from the circle of King Arthur, appears and asks what is probably a ritual question, thereby lifting the fateful spell which is on the king and his realm.

Seen from a poetic angle and as part of the framework of a fantastic romance of chivalry, it all sounds fairly acceptable. Without taking into account what was later made of Chretien's work, a great number of problems still remain to be solved for anyone who is determined to unravel all the mysteries. Not only Perceval, but also the reader is unable to understand what the Grail and the lance really mean and what their purpose might be. Somewhere we feel they must be related to a great, even awe-inspiring, mystery and, despite the unfathomable nature of the mystery, we feel completely spellbound. Nowhere is our curiosity satisfied by the author in the text itself: he whets our appetite but then does nothing to appease our hunger. It is nevertheless possible to imagine without too much effort the complete scenario of *Perceval*. This will help us on our way for a time but provides no real answer to the true, deeper nature of the Grail. It is obviously a potent magical talisman, but further . . . ? The question is answered partly by Robert de Boron, whose work was repeatedly plundered by the inexhaustible, meandering followers of de Troyes. Robert was a poet from Burgundy, in the service of Gauthier de Montbéliard who was to die in the Crusades. A reasonable assumption is that de Boron, like so many Frenchmen in the Angevin era, spent some time in England where he would have enjoyed the protection of Henry II. He apparently had other sources than Chrétien, unless Chrétien still had a lot of surprises *in petto*, to be sprung on us before the end of his *Perceval*, had his death not prevented it. Be that as it may, de Boron introduced in about 1200, in the title figure of his *Joseph of Arimathaea* – presumably the first book of a trilogy which is unknown in its totality and was probably never completed – a completely new character in the Arthurian literature.

Robert de Boron was no great artist but neither did he make things easy for himself. On reading Chrétien's *Perceval*, he seems to have been deeply impressed by the unspecified Grail, as yet completely removed from any Eucharistic meaning. In the first sequel to *Perceval*, however, de Boron was struck by a new element. The anonymous *continuateur* here tells the further story of Gawain and has him arrive in the castle of the Grail. He too sees the strange procession and learns that the bleeding lance was that which, according to the legend, the Roman soldier Longinus used to pierce Jesus' side. At the time, this story appeared as particularly topical since the somewhat unlikely tale that this weapon had been found in Antioch during the first Crusade (1098) had been going the rounds for some time. Naturally, this caused the Grail to appear in a completely different, and purely religious, context. This is probably the reason why de Boron started looking for answers in the Christian tradition. He immersed himself in the study of the Apocryphal *Gospel of Nicodemus*,

*Therewithal the tempest ceased
and passed, that afore was
marvellous to hear.*

And as Sir Bors looked over his head he saw a sword like silver naked hoving over his head, and the clearness thereof smote so in his eyes that as at that time Sir Bors was blind . . .

which was not officially recognized by the church, and more especially in that part which is known as the *Acts of Pilate*. Meanwhile there is no need to demonstrate that his Joseph of Arimathaea also appears in the four canonical gospels. He was a mysterious follower of Jesus who, with Pilate's consent, took Jesus' body down from the cross and laid it with loving care in a tomb that had been destined for himself. This was the end of Joseph's official role but his intervention nevertheless gave rise to a number of pious legends which de Boron used as a point of departure. In the dish from which Jesus had eaten the Paschal lamb during the Last Supper, Joseph of Arimathaea collects the last drops of the Saviour's blood when He is taken down from the cross. As a result, this vessel becomes a very holy relic – sometimes confused with the beaker from which the Saviour drank the wine; it is called the Grail by Robert, in imitation of Chrétien, and gradually in the literature begins to look more and more like a chalice. While Joseph remains in Judaea, his brother-in-law, his brother-in-law's family and a number of trusty followers take the Grail under their protection and leave the country. Preaching the faith, they head west, cross the sea from Gaul and eventually arrive with the Grail at a place in England which is called the Vale of Avalon. The invaluable object has now arrived in Britain. There was still no connection with the stories of the Round Table; but the seed that will give rise to an impressive literary, popular and religious tradition had been sown.

Anyone who tries to follow in King Arthur's footsteps – as is the aim of this book – is constantly being reminded that he is travelling through a highly complex world. Historical facts whose accuracy is difficult to assess, a partly courtly, partly religiously coloured literature and a far from negligible popular tradition constantly overlap. Robert de Boron is the first to connect the Grail with a mysterious region named Avalon. The name Avalon had in fact already been used by Geoffrey of Monmouth without any reference whatsoever to the Grail. After the battle of Camlann, he says: 'Arthur himself, our illustrious king, was fatally wounded and taken to the Island of Avalon, so that his wounds could be healed there.' We learn more about this land when Geoffrey's *Vita Merlini* (1150) appears. Avalon is then made to coincide with the Gorgon Islands and the Hesperides in the Atlantic Ocean. Avalon thus takes its place in ancient geography and is situated in the same area as Homer's Elyseum. Geoffrey derived his mythical geographical knowledge from Pliny's *De Rerum Natura* and was in fact referring to Madeira and the Azores. These islands were regarded as the kingdom of the dead in the ancient world but could sometimes for a while be the abode of someone who had not yet died. What we have here is an Indo-European component which also seems to belong to the Celtic tradition. Whoever, be he dead or alive, sets foot in this world will – like Odysseus on Circe's island – enjoy the company of very loving and compliant female characters related to the fairies, and therefore supernatural. Mythical islands such as these are mainly destined for the departed who, however, continue to feel and behave as though they are alive, but for ever freed from illness, age and care. As far as Arthur is concerned, it is Morgan, his half-sister and one-time lover, who will look after him here.

A number of linguists explain the name Avalon

So the noise sprang in Arthur's court that Launcelot had gotten a child upon Elaine, the daughter of King Pelles, wherefore Queen Guenever was wroth, and gave many rebukes to Sir Launcelot, and called him false knight.

Then King Arthur brought her on her way with more than an hundred knights through a forest.

by referring to the Celtic demigod Avallach who reigns over the underworld. The word can also be linked to the Celtic *aval*. This is recognized in *apple*, a fruit with associations of knowledge, fertility and immortality. Avalon could therefore mean *Apple Orchard* and, as such, be a reference to the classical Garden of the Hesperides with its golden apples and all the other Elysian associations. A majority of linguists, however, seem to give preference to the name Avallach and take the line that there may have been something like a kingdom of Avallach which gradually became Avalon. What may have happened is that the Breton bards and, more especially, the French minstrels, who were instrumental in bringing the Arthurian material to the Continent, did not really know what to do with the name Avallach and substituted a place-name which occurs in France, namely Avalon, the pretty little town in Burgundy.

Meanwhile, one should not lose sight of the fact that, in de Boron's time, the place where he situated Joseph of Arimathaea and his friends' arrival in Britain with the Grail is in fact called Glastonbury. This is a modest market town, which today has something like 7000 inhabitants and is situated some 25 miles south of Bristol. Around 1200, Glastonbury would have been called something like Glaestingaburg, which may point to the possible settlement of an Anglo-Saxon Glaestinclan in which it was thought the word *glass* could be recognized. Its location in an area of marshland, together with an association of ideas rooted in popular etymology, turned Glaestingaburg into *Glass Island*, which in turn was related to Ynis-Witrin, regarded as the original Celtic name. The appearance of the notion of glass in this toponymic circle fits perfectly into the British world of fantasy and need not be explained with reference to the blues, the greens and the sometimes misty atmosphere which here dominate the landscape. The fact is that, in the Celtic tradition, particular fairy-tale places are associated with glass, sometimes meaning crystal. There are mythological glass hills, bridges, islands, houses, castles and even ships. They all belong to the otherworld and are peopled and used by unreal creatures. Apart from the fact that in the ancient world there is something magical about glass because of its transparency – something that, psychologically, seems to point to the world of ghosts – stories of the kind that are now being referred to may also have arisen from concrete phenomena. A number of hill-forts from the old Celtic world are described as vitrified and, more simply, as glass fortresses. Stone defence walls and earthworks appear to have been exposed to fire and seem, as a result, to have hardened.

After some hesitation, the archaeologists have arrived at the conclusion that the Celts, by means of a technique whose details still escape us, had mastered the art of heating the enormous ramparts of their defence works in such a way as to cause vitrification. Besides a number of hill-forts in France and Scotland, the phenomenon has also been encountered in Belgian Limburg, close to the Dutch border, with the discovery of the headquarters of Ambiorix, one of the leaders in the war against the legions of Caesar. It is obvious that 'glass castles' of that kind must have exerted a strong influence on popular imagination and given rise to many legends.

It is a well-known fact that the prehistoric

*And then they rode from country
to country, in forests, and in
wilderness, and in wastes . . .*

I wot full well, said Sir Ector, what it is; it is an Holy vessel that is borne by a maiden, and therein is part of the holy blood of our Lord Jesu Christ, blessed mote he be. But it may not be seen, said Sir Ector, but if it be by a perfect man.

inhabitants of the area around Glastonbury made delicate glass objects, an element which has been used as an argument to explain the *glass/witrin* component in the place-names of Glastonbury and Ynis-Witrin. It can however, even in the best possible case, only constitute a secondary, albeit fortuitous element. The fact is that there is ample reason to believe that the concept of glass includes a major spiritual component. The town, no longer an island, has become a centre with strong mythical associations, where dream and reality intermingle. In what follows, therefore, fantasy and reality are indissolubly linked. This is in keeping with the attitude of Freeman, a nineteenth-century historian: 'It is not necessary to believe that the Glastonbury legends correspond to reality,' he says, 'but the existence of such legends is in itself an extremely important fact.' These legends caused the small provincial town, the centre of what is both a pretty and peaceful agricultural area, to grow into a place of pilgrimage attracting thousands.

Glastonbury is on the border between the Somerset hills and the plain stretching out towards the Bristol Channel in the northwest where the Severn flows into the sea. Except for the hills in the distance, particularly to the northeast, the landscape could be that of the Low Countries *polder* area. Remarkably enough, the area is called the *Poldens* and is protected by dikes against the high tides in the Bristol Channel. In prehistoric times, this was an impressive area of tidal lakes where man had settled as early as 3000 BC. In the winter the area undoubtedly looked bleak. In the summer, however, it looked attractive with its reeds, willows, oaks, ash, wild roses, brambles, blackthorn and hazel bushes, as well as its

buttercups, water-lilies, marguerites and other wild flowers, in sharp contrast with the nearby higher-lying landscape. Archaeologists have discovered a couple of extensive pile-villages in the area, dating from the Iron Age, when the fairy-tale king Cymbeline, known to us through Shakespeare's play, was reigning over Britain. Whenever possible, the inhabitants laid wattle causeways, sometimes miles long, that led to the surrounding pastures and fields and used canoes made from hollowed-out tree-trunks for fishing. Safe dwelling-places like these pile-villages gave rise to a prosperous economy and a fairly high culture of which the artisanal products can now be admired in the museums of Taunton and Glastonbury itself. The connection between Glastonbury – and therefore Avalon – and the otherworld was established later. It is possible that the inhabitants of the lake-settlements buried their dead in the somewhat higher-lying areas, which include the present town. Ferrying the dead across the water, which was also considered a barrier against the spirits, corresponded precisely to Celtic ideas on the realm of the dead, which also meant eternal life. The prehistoric Glastonbury, then an island, surrounded by what amounted to a lake and, as such, called Ynis-Witrin, was an impressive place in those days. It was dominated by the Tor, a striking, steep, conical hill 150 metres high, that looks something like a pyramid and presents a perfectly unreal appearance. At the foot, there is a well with reddish water, now called the Chalice Well. Worth mentioning is the presence of what for the druids would have been an important oak grove and oak-lined avenue. Both of these were felled in 1906 with the exception of a few trees at a place which is now called Stonedown. Some of

And in the meanwhile came Sir Percivale de Galis and Sir Ector de Maris under that castle that was called the Joyous Isle. And as they beheld that gay castle they would have gone to that castle, but they might not for the broad water, and bridge could they find none.

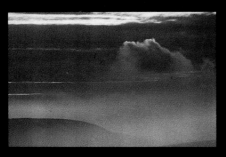

O Jesu, said King Arthur, I marvel for what cause ye, Sir Launcelot, went out of your mind. I and many others deem it was for the love of fair Elaine, the daughter of King Pelles, by whom ye are noised that ye have gotten a child, and his name is Galahad, and men say he shall do marvels.

these trees appeared to have at least 2000 rings. Since the druids really did correspond to historical reality, it is reasonable to assume that Ynis-Witrin had, from time immemorial, been a sanctuary for them and their followers, giving access to Annwn, the Celtic hereafter and underworld, situated either over the sea or under the earth. Mention of the druids does not necessarily mean that it all started with them. In *Perlesvaus*, popularized in English as *The High Story of the Holy Grail*, an Arthurian romance (1225), which seems to be set in the area of Glastonbury, there is a significant but grim passage. The son of King Gurgulan is killed by a giant, but his body is recovered by Sir Gawain. The unhappy father, Gurgulan, converts himself to Christianity out of gratitude. This, however, does not prevent the tragic event from being followed by a frightening ritual. The young man's body is hacked into pieces, boiled in a cauldron and eaten by those present. This amazing example of cannibalism most certainly has roots that reach far back into prehistory, a phenomenon which later will frequently have to be taken into account.

Furthermore, it appears that the area of Ynis-Witrin still evokes heathen reminiscences as late as the Middle Ages. In a saint's life about the monk Collen, we learn how he is invited to visit Gwyn ap Nud, the king of the elves, possibly Avallach, who lives in a luxurious castle on the Tor, which presumably means *in* the hill itself. With the help of a liberal sprinkling of holy water, the saintly hermit manages to drive out what is obviously an underworld figure and his dissolute companions. This brings us back again to Arthur. None other than Chrétien de Troyes tells us in his *Lancelot* (1168) that Guinevere is

abducted by the king of the realm of shadows and kept safe on the far from unpleasant '*Isle de Voire*', i.e., the Glass Island. The kidnapper this time is Maléagant but can certainly be identified as Melwas and the prison is clearly on the Tor.

The story was not completely new. It is encountered in the previously mentioned *Vita Gildae* by Caradoc of Llancarfan, which appeared shortly after 1100. In this work, Melwas, the king of Somerset, has abducted Guinevere and holds her captive on the same Tor in '*Glastonia, id est Urbs Vitrae*'. In what follows, Caradoc repeats quite clearly that the place concerned is *Ynisgutrin* or *Glastigberi*, also called the Glass Island. Arthur hurries to the rescue with his army but does not get through the marshes. So, our old friend Gildas, who is then staying at Glastonbury Abbey, is called in. He is apparently not yet irreconcilably involved in a conflict with the king, or perhaps is prepared to forget about the quarrel for a moment. Whatever the case may be, he acts as a go-between to negotiate Guinevere's release, which is after all no more than his duty as a Christian. Arthur's relationship with Glastonbury appears here for the first time – the importance of this will soon become clear.

It is no coincidence that the Tor plays an important role in stories of this kind. From 1962 to 1964, excavations were conducted on the crown of this mysterious hill by the archaeologist Philip Ranz. The results showed that, in the Arthurian period, there had been a small fortified settlement, probably the residence of a local tribal chief who might quite possibly have been the Melwas from the legends. Ranz does not take the offered opportunity to bridge the gap that would take us from the name Melwas to Gwyn ap

And I will that ye wit that this same day shall the adventures of the Sangreal, that is called the Holy Vessel, begin.

Nud or possibly Avallach with its underworld tone. What is important is the chapel that was erected here in the early Middle Ages and was later replaced by a modest Norman church; it was destroyed by an earthquake and only the squat, truncated tower survives. Both chapel and church were dedicated to St Michael, who was, like St George, the enemy of the dragon of disbelief. This steep hilltop is in fact a highly unlikely spot for a place of worship, but the name St Michael immediately reminds one of the many Christian sanctuaries that were systematically built with the explicit approval of the religious authorities at places where the heathen gods had previously been present. This too seems to indicate that the Tor was once connected with threats from hell and consequently with the Celtic underworld.

The mysterious nature of the Tor is unmistakable and considerably exceeds the possibilities of what a superstitious population could read into what is basically a strangely shaped hill if left to their own devices, with no help from tradition. No archaeological insight is necessary to notice that the sides of the hill present a terraced appearance. Closer examination reveals that this in fact consists of a single pathway that winds its way to the top in a series of seven circuits, provided here and there with ingenious detours so as to form a labyrinth. The labyrinth is in itself an odyssey rich in psychological and religious significance. It was present as a symbolic representation among the neolithic peoples (from 4000 BC onwards) who spread westwards through Europe from the Mediterranean area and who were to become the builders of the large megalithic structures at Carnac in Brittany, Avebury and Stonehenge. Such labyrinths, figuring repeatedly in the form of spirals on menhirs or rock surfaces, as in the 'Rock Valley' near Tintagel, provided the basic pattern for folk dances that are still performed in England and which have an underlying ritual meaning. Under Christianity they are retained in the tiling pattern of certain cathedral floors, where they are assumed to have represented a miniature pilgrimage of prayer to be performed on one's knees. Spirals, with what, in origin, was probably an extensive cosmic significance, possibly connected with vague, intuitive imaginings of how original matter could begin to order itself in the endless space of creation, have remained with us up to the present time. In Flanders and probably elsewhere it was until recently the custom for the rural housewife to complete the weekly cleaning by sprinkling sand over the paved floor, sometimes in the form of skilfully arranged spirals. The spiral pattern is also preserved in what is predominantly a little girls' activity, namely hopscotch. It is also found in original board games, like the royal game of geese, in which the game consists of negotiating an obstacle-strewn route to arrive at a given goal, thereby reducing the quests of the knights of the Round Table to parlour proportions.

In the stories that we have been considering, Glastonbury is not definitely identified with the place-name Avalon. The references, however, to an otherworldly monarch Gwyn, Melwas or Méléagant are significant in this respect. Like Rhadamantos in Homer's *Odyssey* and the Celts' *Avallach*, Gwyn reigns over a 'Summer Country' and a 'Glass Island' with clearly Elysian connotations. This tradition reached both the hagiographer Caradoc of Llancarfan in Wales (shortly after 1100) and the poet Chrétien in Champagne or Poitou (1168). A centuries-old

Then came King Arthur unto Galahad and said: Sir, ye be welcome, for ye shall move many good knights to the quest of the Sangreal, and ye shall achieve that never knights might bring to an end.

And, Sir king, Nacien, the hermit, sendeth thee word, that thee shall befall the greatest worship that ever befell king in Britain; and I say you wherefore, for this day the Sangreal appeared in thy house and feed thee and all thy fellowship of the Round Table.

tradition has it that Glastonbury, long a particularly strange sort of island, surrounded by marshes and rivers, is a somewhat special place, where the visible and the invisible cannot be distinguished. That Geoffrey of Monmouth was apparently thinking of another, more Mediterranean or even oceanic, Avalon, seems to have no echo in the Arthurian literature.

When Robert de Boron in 1200 had Joseph of Arimathaea's friends from Jerusalem bring the Grail specifically to Avalon, in other words to Glastonbury, he may have had serious reasons for his choice. He certainly knew that there was a Cistercian abbey there, generally regarded as the most important in England, and whose superb present-day ruins with their mystic atmosphere have given the town its greatest attraction for visitors. In Boron's day, this abbey was the religious, intellectual and even economic centre of Somerset or at least well on the way to it. Ten years before Robert was to start his Grail book, a remarkable discovery had been made – in 1190 (not in 1191, as the official version still has it). Henry II had died in 1189. Several years previously he had given Abbot Robert de Sully a strange message. On his travels in Wales he had been told by a bard that Arthur was buried very deep under Glastonbury Abbey. This had been kept secret in order to protect the last resting place of the famous king from Saxon desecration in the event of a possible military breakthrough.

This is worth looking at in some detail. Its complexities are in fact reminiscent of the best of Agatha Christie. The bards, who in twelfth-century Wales still enjoyed considerable prestige, were part of an institutionalized, more or less hermetic caste, with various hierarchic degrees and a desire to impress with the

mysteries of its art. It cannot be excluded that the bards, possibly in view of the mythical material employed in their earliest period, as well as through their connections with Welsh-nationalist resistance first to the Anglo-Saxons and afterwards to the Normans, may have preserved certain strictly kept secrets. Geoffrey Ashe proposes the rather romantic but not unreasonable idea that after the Battle of Camlann Arthur's death and burial might have been kept secret for political reasons, which could consequently have given rise to the legend of his immortality. In bardic society, comparable in some ways to freemasonry and still permeated by vague druidic memories, one of its secrets may have been the place where Arthur was laid to rest, chosen so that it should not be discovered by the Saxons or other possible foreign invaders. In the Welsh *Black Book of Camarthen* from the twelfth century, which is in fact a compilation of considerably older texts, there is a *Song of the Graves* in which those of three famous heroes are mentioned. It is then stated that Arthur's grave is a secret or should be a secret. The text is fairly ambiguous – deliberately? – and therefore difficult to translate. From the different interpretations that the Arthurian specialist Ashe has collated, he concludes that the poet seems to be in on the secret, while, bound by some promise or other, wanting to preserve it.

Now imagine the situation of our bard performing for Henry II. Deeply impressed by the honour, possibly deliberately made drunk, just plain overexcited or as result of close questioning, he allows his mouth to run away with him and refers to Arthur's burial place. The king is listening attentively and passes the message on to the abbot of Glastonbury,

Now, said the King, I am sure at this quest of the Sangreal shall all ye of the Table Round depart, and never shall I see you again whole together; therefore I will see you all whole together in the meadow of Camelot to joust and to tourney, that after your death men may speak of it that such good knights were wholly together such a day.

Then anon they heard cracking and crying of thunder, that them thought the place should all to-drive.

naturally with the express wish that something should be done about it. His death would obviously cause some delay but, armed with the information furnished by Henry, the Glastonbury monks start serious digging in 1190.

A well-documented account of this 'archaeological' campaign can be found in two works by the historian Giraldus Cambriensis (Gerald of Wales, 1145–1223): the reports, in his *De Principes Instructione* (1194) and his later *Speculum Ecclesia* (1216), show how great an importance he attached to it. This is what he has to tell us after staying at Glastonbury in 1192 and 1193.

Between two pyramids mentioned by the bard, presumably old Celtic memorials like the Tristan pillar in Cornwall, the monks need only to dig down a metre or two on the south side of the Lady Chapel in the old monastery cemetery to find a stone slab. On the underside of the slab a lead cross is fixed, about 30 centimetres long and provided with an inscription. Gerald's copy of the text reads: 'Here, on the Isle of Avalon, lies buried the renowned King Arthur, together with Guinevere, his second wife.' After this auspicious start, the monks dig bravely on until, at a depth of about five metres, they find a hollowed-out tree trunk containing the skeletons of a man and a woman. The man turns out to have been a giant of a fellow on whose skull the scars of ten wounds can be seen, one of which was clearly the cause of death. Close to the woman's frail skeleton, a blonde braid is found, which crumbles to the touch. In the following quotation from Gerald, he reveals himself with respect to the incident of the braid as a subtle psychologist, almost as a Freudian *avant la lettre*, which lends his story a striking note of truthfulness:

'In the grave a braid of woman's hair was found, blond and pleasing to behold, very skilfully curled and plaited, and undoubtedly belonging to Arthur's wife, buried here together with her husband. The moment that one of the crowd of monks caught sight of this braid, he leapt into the deep grave and attempted to seize it before anyone else. This was a shameless act, which showed little respect for the dead. Now this monk . . . a silly, reckless and undisciplined fellow . . . threw himself into the pit, tantamount to a symbol of that hell from which none of us shall escape. He was determined to obtain possession of this braid of woman's hair before anyone else could do so and touch it with his hands. This was a clear sign of his lustful thoughts, for women's hair is a trap for weak natures . . .'

With respect to Gerald's description of this piece of hair-fetishism we can adopt the French reaction of *cela ne s'invente pas*: that's not fiction. Unless of course the writer is credited with as much imagination as the commentators who suspect Henry II of having given orders that this sensual braid should be placed in the thoroughly faked grave. Since my imagination won't stretch that far, I find Gerald's version by and large a fairly credible story. Anyway, it is possible to assume that it was in fact Arthur and Guinevere whose mortal remains were carefully preserved by the monks. In 1278 these remains were provided with a black marble sepulchral monument opposite the church's high altar, where they remained until Henry VIII's dissolution of the abbey in 1539, when the bones were dispersed. In the present ruins, the location

*In the midst of this blast entered a
sunbeam more clearer by seven
times than ever they saw day, and
all they were alighted of the grace
of the Holy Ghost.*

When Sir Galahad heard this he thanked God, and took his horse; and he had not ridden but half a mile, he saw in a valley afore him a strong castle with deep ditches, and there ran beside it a fair river that hight Severn . . .

of this monument is indicated by a fenced-off rectangle in the grass with the green sign that is customary in England for ancient monuments.

The lead cross was recovered but later lost again, although the historian Camden saw it in 1607 and made a drawing of it. His version of the inscription does not correspond to what Gerald wrote, reading: 'Here lies buried the renowned King Arthur on the Isle of Avalon.' Camden's drawing is presumably correct, but for the confusing second wife mentioned by Gerald we have to take the possibility of the text's running round the obverse into account – unless Camden made his drawing afterwards and his memory failed him.

According to Beram Saklatvala, Arthur did in fact marry twice. His first marriage was to a Christian Saxon princess called Wenever or Winiver. Since the couple did not get on, Arthur sent her away and married Guinevere. But 'Winever' is surely identical with 'Guinevere'? The medieval poets were embarrassed by the problem as well, thereby giving rise to the stubborn tradition of two, or in Wales even three, Guineveres. The two namesakes are explained away in the thirteenth-century English *Arthour and Merlin* in the following none-too-convincing way. The first, and therefore the genuine, Guinevere was the daughter of one Leodogrance, who later fathered a bastard daughter on the wife of his seneschal, who was also baptized Guinevere and who appears in the story from time to time. It is also thought that after the adventure with Melwas, in which Guinevere may have been more accomplice than victim, the marriage would have had to be officially reconsecrated, so giving rise to later misunderstandings.

I would suggest the following solution. From Guinevere's adventure with Mordred it appears that she must have been much younger than Arthur. The memory of a first wife, probably less radiantly beautiful, less lively and adventurous than her successor, was in time lost and only that of the more tragic Guinevere was finally fixed by tradition. It's as simple as that.

In the meantime, we have come across the first direct identification of Glastonbury with Avalon. It is obvious that an epigraphic document like the cross yields considerably more matter for controversy than the discovery of Arthur's burial place, in itself sensational enough. Indeed, the whole episode is later considered to be extremely doubtful. For the nineteenth century in particular, with its rationalist and materialist sciences, this is an understandable reflex. Its historians are little inclined to ally themselves with dubious, medieval and – from the Anglican viewpoint – popish writers and their pious or fantastic ravings, so that the affair is reduced to the following.

In 1184, the abbey suffered a great fire. Rebuilding would naturally cost a lot of money. The unexpected death of Henry II had cut off all hope of the support promised from that direction, while his successor was deeply involved in a crusade. Consequently, the monks fabricated the story of a secret that a bard had passed on to the late king. In the cemetery they organized the semblance of a large-scale search and broadcast the attractive tale of a cross, a coffin, skeletons, a skull with a fatal wound and, last but not least, a blonde braid of woman's hair with Freudian overtones. They then sat back and waited for the pilgrims to Arthur's bones to arrive from all points of the compass and fill the coffers.

*But Sir Launcelot rode
overthwart and endlong in a wild
forest, and held no path but as
wild adventure led him.*

Then he returned and came to his horse and did off his saddle and bridle, and let him pasture . . .

It reads like some jolly, anticlerical, swashbuckling romance, but as an historical hypothesis it misses a few points. It seems, for example, highly improbable that the clerics should count on collecting the necessary funds from an appeal to the limited resources of pilgrims who themselves often had difficulty making ends meet, and in many cases meant more loss than profit. Moreover, Glastonbury was one of the richest abbeys in England, possessing extensive estates, fertile fields and valuable real estate. A common joke of the period has it that the abbot of Glastonbury would only have to marry the prioress of Shaftebury to possess more land than the king of England. In these circumstances a fire need not be an insurmountable financial disaster, to be faced with rather improvised begging. If it had really been their intention to relieve pilgrims of their money, the monks could easily have done so without recourse to the stunt with King Arthur, who, for outsiders at least, had so far had no apparent connection with the abbey, except via the hagiographies, which of necessity were primarily intended for the clergy itself. The abbey cemetery did have a reputation as the burial place of several prominent saints. The 'discovery' and exhibition of their remains would have been financially at least as interesting as those of Arthur, who was unfavourably viewed by the clergy and, therefore, theoretically, by all Christians.

In 1962, the earth under the cemetery was scientifically excavated. On what is traditionally considered to be the location of Arthur's burial site it did in fact seem that once a deep pit had been dug and afterwards filled in. It is, however, necessary to bear in mind that the monks are still suspected of having arranged the whole thing, which they would not have spoiled for a bit of spadework. They would, then, have buried, according to some sources, a dugout canoe with its contents, so as to dig it up again triumphantly, including part of Guinevere's coiffure.

An experienced worker like Professor Leslie Alcock, who excavated Cadbury Castle, shrugs his shoulders with a smile at this theory, thought up at the desk by historians and literary specialists ignorant of archaeological techniques. He seems to smirk particularly at the idea of a Celtic chieftain and his wife, laid to rest 1000 years before in a tree trunk or dugout canoe, being dug up elsewhere and used by the cunning monks to give substance to their fake grave. 'The only suitable commentary on this is,' he says, 'that not a single present-day archaeologist would have the faintest idea of where to find such a burial.'

Professor Alcock has also looked at the problem of the lead cross, paying particular attention to the letters on it. These do not correspond to the letters used in Arthur's time, i.e., around 500, but neither do they correspond to the letters that one would expect from the time of the alleged fabrication (1190). They can best be situated in the Saxon world of around 950, which apparently leaves the matter even more inexplicable than before. It is, however, precisely here that the answer to the puzzle lies, according to Alcock. In the middle of the tenth century, Abbot Dunstan had the cemetery, which had become too small, covered in a layer of loam to a depth of several metres so that it could continue to be used. Arthur's coffin would not have been touched, but when every trace of the grave had, in spite of its acknowledged importance, been

And within an hour and less he bare him four days' journey thence, until he came to a rough water the which roared, and his horse would have borne him into it.

By that Sir Percivale had abiden there till mid-day he saw a ship came rowing in the sea as all the wind of the world had driven it.

buried under all that loam, the new stone was placed in position, together with its inscription from 950. The cemetery level was later raised further, burying the new stone in its turn. Alcock also considers the possibility that Arthur's original grave might have been provided with a pillar similar to the Tristan pillar, with an inscription such as 'Hic sepultus jacit Arturius' ('Here lies Arthur') or something similar. This pillar would have been replaced by the familiar stone slab when the level of the cemetery was raised, together with the lead cross bearing a longer inscription, apparently better suited to the folk tradition by which the *dux bellorum* had in the meantime become a famous king who was buried in Avalon. As already pointed out, Guinevere's status as Arthur's second wife need present no problem, whereas this specific mention does lend the whole thing a certain degree of truthfulness, on condition, that is, that Giraldus Cambriensis read the inscription correctly.

Since some researchers appear to have realized that the hypothetical stunt by avaricious monks carried very little conviction in itself, they attempted to underline their view by means of another, this time a political, argument. While Henry Plantagenet, whose story was apparently so easily believed in the monastery, was still alive, the intention was to lend the monarch a helping hand. The king had always had great difficulty in imposing his authority on the fanatically nationalist Welsh. With their fertile imaginations, the Welsh activists were almost genetically inclined to confuse their dreams with reality. They believed (or at any rate spread the idea) that King Arthur would someday return to drive out the Normans. For Henry II it was

important to put an end to this sort of nationalist chimera by means of the discovery of Arthur's remains. Once his death had been clearly established for all time, it would certainly no longer be a hindrance to have his praises sung by the poets as a symbol of the ideal prince, now definitely represented by the Angevin dynasty. This would explain why the monks were persuaded to perform a fake exhumation with all the accompanying fuss.

This is certainly an interesting view, which is to some extent confirmed by Gerald, at least as far as the basic point of the exercise is concerned. After the discovery of the grave, Gerald does in fact write: 'Many stories are told and many legends are created around King Arthur and his mysterious end. The Britons, in their stupidity, maintain that he is still alive.' At the same time, the writer is in no doubt at all that Arthur was indeed a historical figure. He is, however, here concerned with publishing the facts: fatally wounded at the Battle of Camlann, he was brought by a noble lady, clearly not a fay but his cousin Morgan (not his incestuous half-sister!) to Avalon, i.e., Glastonbury, and was buried in the cemetery there. 'Consequently,' as Gerald patronizingly adds, 'the credulous Britons and their bards thought up the story of Arthur's body being brought to the Isle of Avalon by a marvellous sorceress, Morgan, in order to heal him of his wounds. According to them, this strong and all-powerful king will return to resume his reign over the Britons.' None of which proves that a forgery was committed in the abbey.

In the beginning of the twelfth century, Caradoc of Llancarfan put the living Arthur, though temporarily deprived of his wife, in the Glastonbury context. Chrétien de Troyes did the

And so she went with the wind roaring and yelling, that it seemed all the water brent after her.

Then looked Launcelot up to the heaven, and him seemed the clouds did open . . .

same in 1168 in his *Lancelot ou le Chevalier à la Charrette* (*Lancelot or the Knight in the Cart*). After the discovery of the notorious grave in 1190, Gerald adds to this (and it is irrelevant that he does this was an admonishing finger in the direction of 'the credulous Britons') the fact that tradition has here transformed him, through the intervention of Morgan the fay, into the inhabitant of another dimension, known as Avalon. Why am I placing so much stress on this?

Giraldus Cambriensis stayed at Glastonbury Abbey in 1192 and 1193 and wrote about this twice, in 1194 and 1216. In 1200 Robert de Boron's *Joseph of Arimathaea*, written in the late 1190s, appeared. The dates are crucially important. Some people claim that Glastonbury would have derived its enormously rich tradition from the Grail romances. After the successful stunt with the fake, or possibly even non-existent, Arthur's grave, so runs their reasoning, the monks really get the bit between their teeth. They encourage the poets to allocate the abbey a central role in all sorts of incredible books, so that, on the basis of the Arthur legends and the presence of the now clearly Christianized Grail, it can develop into a mystical and historical centre. This line of reasoning clearly aims to underline the purely imaginary nature of King Arthur.

It is, however, equally clear that the Glastonbury legend, in no way diminished by Gerald's scepticism with respect to its supernatural aspects, but rather consecrated by him in the fullest sense of the words as a living tradition, had already been in existence for some time before de Boron in 1200 wrote down the story of the Grail and its arrival in Avalon.

It is therefore incorrect to assume that

Glastonbury Abbey cunningly annexed the Arthur material from elsewhere by means of the identification of Avalon with the neighbouring town. Undoubtedly, the abbey did, in time, support, stimulate and help disseminate the literature in which this material was included, in all innocence of the heathen soil in which it was rooted. Meanwhile, it does seem clear that Glastonbury contributed new elements to the archetypal Arthurian material. These belonged, however, to a local tradition that considerably pre-dated a story that de Boron borrowed from the *Gospel of Nicodemus* sometime around 1200. The French literary historian Jean Marx is convinced that de Boron, although writing reasonably knowledgeably about the Grail, could tell the Glastonbury clerics nothing that they did not already know. He regards Robert as having derived his material from texts that he had found in the library of the abbey itself. It can be said with some degree of grandiloquence that Glastonbury, after the discovery of Arthur and Guinevere's grave, began to reveal its secrets.

What were these secrets?

The first of them, the presence in the abbey of Arthur's last resting place, has already been dealt with at length. There is a fair chance that Abbot Robert de Sully did not even need the king's hint, since he would know well enough on the basis of the quasi-official local accounts handed down by successive prelates – but kept secret from the outside world – that the famous *dux bellorum* was buried in the abbey cemetery. It is, furthermore, not impossible that he should have had access to documents describing in detail the events after the Battle of Camlann; how one dramatic night the body of the dead or dying hero was brought part of the way along the old Roman road and

And then mounted upon his horse, and rode into a forest, and held no highway. And as he looked afore him he saw a fair plain . . .

And so rode into a deep valley, and there he saw a river and an high mountain.

through the marshes from Cadbury Castle to Glastonbury, to be buried there, surrounded by his last companions, who swore themselves to secrecy around the bier or by the open grave. He could perhaps have read how the body of the lifeless Guinevere was later brought from the convent at Amesbury, where she had gone into retreat and become a prioress, to Glastonbury to be buried alongside her husband.

We can further easily imagine that the monks would tell and re-tell the same tall stories that still crop up today in the Somerset folklore. Sometimes a nocturnal passer-by will make out a giant, ghostly figure with a bloodied head, staring hollow-eyed at the Brue as it flows past Pomparles bridge. It is, of course, Arthur, come back again to the place where he once had Sir Bedivere throw Excalibur into the water, returning the sword to the Lady of the Lake. No less lugubrious is the ghostly procession that winds its way to the abbey in the pale glow of smoking torches, bringing Guinevere's dead body from Amesbury.

Should we dismiss *a priori* the idea that such historical and legendary traditions were preserved here? It answers a human need that closed communities should keep certain secrets, real or fictitious, with what amounts to ritual dedication. There was, moreover, yet another tradition in Glastonbury, with an apparently wide currency before 1200 and so clearly not a secret, but which formed a sort of mental smokescreen that hid the true mysteries from sight.

When the Saxons, already long converted to Christianity, finally moved into Glastonbury in 658, it appears that the monks were unable to provide any sort of information about the founding of their abbey for their new masters,

who were doubtless curious about things in this hitherto completely Celtic world with its separate, largely Irish-inspired Christianity. Did they want to keep the secret of Arthur's grave from his old arch-enemies, the Saxons?

Let's leave the wood to itself for a moment and pay attention to the trees. The aim is to find a reasonable answer to the question of how Robert de Boron should come to write a book in which he has the friends and relations of Joseph of Arimathaea arriving in Glastonbury shortly after Christ's Passion. If he took this from a tradition or a document in the abbey itself, this would mean that his source referred to an extremely early Christian settlement in Ynis-Witrin. The poet was presumably attracted by the fact that the founders of the abbey would have been disciples of the living Jesus Christ, who had seen the drama of Golgotha with their own eyes. The essential point is whether there was such a legend in Glastonbury around, or rather long before, 1200.

It is accepted that the abbey of Ynis-Witrin stemmed in any case from a particularly early Christian settlement. Hermits are said to have established themselves in the marshes around a primitive, mud-walled church. Irish missionaries, including St Patrick, are reputed to have organized the small community later on, endowing it with a monastic rule. This theory involves a fair number of historical and chronological improbabilities and is clearly inspired by wishful thinking. It seems therefore not unreasonable to look at the question, however contrary this may be to the usual practice, in the general context of the historically acceptable account of how England was converted to Christianity.

Thus as Ector and Gawaine rode
more than eight days. And on a
Saturday they found an old
chapel, the which was wasted that
there seemed no man thither
repaired . . .

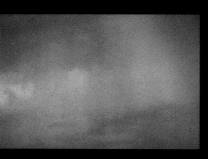

ir Gawaine him seemed he came
nto a meadow full of herbs and
owers . . .

We know that early Christian writers like Tertullian and Origen noted in about 200 that some inhabitants of the British Isles were Christians. Later, in the sixth century, we can read in the works of Gildas that Christianity had come to Britain no later than the reign of Tiberius. Since Tiberius died in AD 37, this would be the latest possible date for the advent of Christianity, which naturally sounds highly improbable. Gildas' dating, however, is obviously faulty, since he also ascribes the event to the time of Boadicea's revolt against the Romans, which did not take place until AD 60. Although his chronology is at fault, Gildas, then, can intend at the very latest the year 60 or thereabouts. He tried, in any case, to situate the advent of Christianity as exactly as possible in the very earliest British history. He did this in a tone that implies that the readers for whom he wrote his *Liber Querulus* would have known about the events he describes.

No less important is the fact that the Anglo-Saxon Bede in his *History of the English Church and People* (731) also has a number of remarkable things to say. According to him, a British king Lucius requested the help of Pope Eleutherus for his conversion to Christianity. 'This pious request was promptly granted and the Britons received the Faith and kept it in all its purity and wholeness until the time of Emperor Diocletian.' There never was a British King Lucius. From the name, it is, however, possible to conclude that what we have here is an influential Roman-British official or possibly a romanized chieftain. That *the*, i.e., *all*, Britons should have received the faith is obviously wishful thinking, but Bede's pronouncement does indicate that Christianity did have some impact on the population. That this should have lasted until the time of Emperor Diocletian is a reliable statement. Towards the end of Diocletian's reign (284–305), in the same period as Carausius' attempted *coup d'état*, a terrible religious persecution was unleashed on the ancient world, probably the worst since Nero. The emperor's first measures in this direction date from 298. One of the consequences in Britain was the martyrdom of St Alban, who ha helped conceal a priest and had been baptized him. The final edict against the Christians followed in 303. Churches were closed, the priests arrested and all copies of the Bible confiscated and publicly burned. This too seem to reflect an archetypal pattern of human intolerance. The moral absurdity is accented by the fact that this persecution, just as with Hitler takeover of power, also involved the accusation that a persecuted minority, this time the Christians, had been setting fire to public buildings.

To make the link with Alban and his conceal priest, it is obvious that numbers of Christians, both priests and laymen, went underground or fled to the countryside. It seems reasonable to assume that one such persecuted group, principally of priests, should have looked, in about the year 300, for a more or less safe refug in the lonely marshes of distant Ynis-Witrin, where according to archaeologists the Roman presence could be felt only very lightly, and tha these refugees should settle there. Did they als feel that they had arrived in the Summer Count of the old Celtic legends, where mortals were al allowed to enter and which might be unconsciously identified with the promised land of the Bible? There would in any case have beer

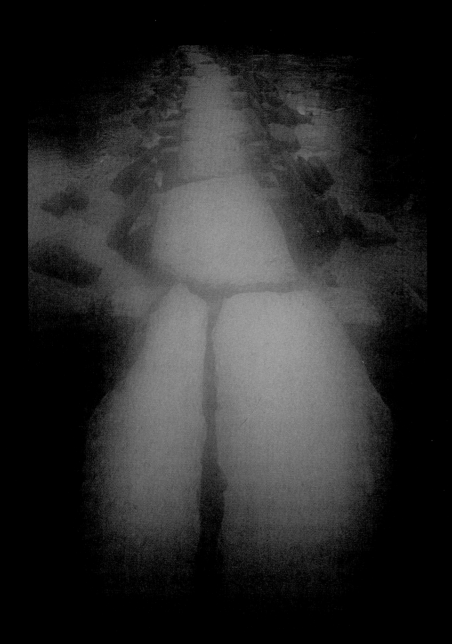

*Sir, said Gawaine, can thou
teach us to any hermit? Here is
one in a little mountain, but it is
so rough there may no horse go
thither, and therefore ye must go
upon foot . . .*

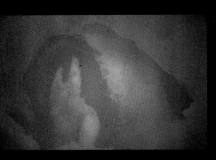

numbers of heathens still living in the area, worshipping their old gods on the Tor and elsewhere. These would be much less dangerous for the refugees than the Roman police spies, much more hospitable and even after a time possible candidates for conversion, which would be a sort of bonus.

In all probability, the monks of Glastonbury Abbey, those latter-day members of a community that had been organized and officially sanctified by Irish preachers, were concealing nothing as they scratched their heads in answer to enquiries by their Saxon colleagues as to the origins of their foundation. Bede, too, says nothing on the subject. With the exception of the strictly necessary religious works, there may have been a complete absence of written sources. Certainly as far as the beginning of the settlement is concerned, when the fight to survive would have been predominant, it is necessary to bear in mind the early Christian tendency known as *millenarism*. This was based on the revelation that Christ had ascended to Heaven and taken his place at God's right hand, but that he would one day return to judge the living and the dead, which was assumed to be in the foreseeable future. This idea lay behind the anchorites, who in Egypt trekked into the desert or who later, in the Celtic-Irish world, sometimes after reckless voyages like that of Brendan, settled in the most inhospitable places, for example Iceland. Here they awaited Christ's return, which they expected in their lifetime. The refugees and their successors at Ynis-Witrin may have been imbued with such ideas, which would have condemned the compilation of day-to-day historical records as a fairly frivolous pastime that was probably counter to God's wishes. The idea of the

1000-year kingdom disappeared in time from Christian theology. By the time, much later, that the pious men of Glastonbury finally started wondering about the foundation of their abbey, the necessary documents would have been lacking and the monks confronted with a mystery.

From Gildas in person, since he was one of them for a time, or from his book, they would learn that the faith was brought to Britain shortly after the death of Christ. That would be about the right time to date the beginnings of their ramshackle old church, or so they might think. The obvious question then is who could have brought the Word here at that time? The early Christian world was shot through with stories of disciples and followers of Jesus who, after the Crucifixion, travelled far and wide to spread the new faith. When Gildas postulates AD 37, or maybe the time of Boadicea's revolt, the monks find this not improbable and decide that, as far as they are concerned, the first missionaries to Britain could well have been eyewitnesses to Christ's teaching and death.

Presumably there were also those abbots who, under the influence of the perennial tension between the Celtic church and Rome, found it all nonsense, but sooner or later the subject would crop up again. Finally, after years of mentally sifting through all the likely Gospel figures to find a suitable candidate to have preached in this distant corner of the world, a clear decision was reached. It could have been none other than Joseph of Arimathaea, the modest, rather anxious and humble soul, who after the tragedy of Golgotha had suddenly overcome the last of his hesitancy to take charge of the body of the dead Christ. According to the *Gospel of*

And so a little from thence he
looked up into a tree, and there
he saw a passing great bird upon
an old tree, and it was passing
dry, without leaves . . .

So by evensong, by adventure he came to a strong tower and an high, and there was he lodged gladly.

Nicodemus, which apparently reached the Celtic world via Ireland, he braved great dangers because of his possession of the bowl in which he had collected the blood of the murdered Messiah. In the company of the apostle Philip, he travelled with this valuable possession first of all to Gaul and then to Britain, where he finally settled with his followers in Ynis-Witrin. Here it must be noted that the story of Philip is in itself a legend that is nowhere mentioned in the most reliable historical document that can be referred to in this respect, *The History of the Franks* by Gregory of Tours (539–594). Still, as a legend, we can allow it in here.

This is a rough synopsis of the story that was arrived at after lengthy debate as a sort of patent of nobility for Glastonbury Abbey and which in time was accepted in complete good faith as historical truth, long before any help would have been called in from an Anglo-Norman minstrel in about 1200. It was presumably recorded in the abbey but there is no direct trace of a text extant, so that we cannot know in what terms it was written or with what particulars it was padded out.

When William of Malmesbury stayed at the abbey in 1125, he browsed about in the books of the library, to which Dunstan had richly contributed. In return for the abbey's hospitality, he then wrote his *De Antiquitate Glastoniensia Ecclesia*. He was presumably not entrusted with the secret of King Arthur's grave, which was unearthed 65 years later, or was himself sworn to secrecy. He did, however, discover a story – already more soberly related by Bede – about the missionaries sent to Britain by Pope Eleutheris in answer to a request from the doubtful King Lucius; their names were apparently Faganus and Deruvianus and they are supposed to have restored the little mud-walled church, which was in a bad state of repair.

This is an indisputable existing tradition, 75 years before de Boron's Grail story and 67 years before Chrétien's *Perceval*. William himself did not believe it. That is of only minor importance for us here, where we are concerned with a tradition, confirmed by our spokesman in 1125, rather than with its historical reliability. It is clearly not an interpolated reference in William's version of the abbey chronicles, since it occurs again in the perfectly reliable *De Gestis Regum Angliae* (*The Deeds of the Kings of England*), written later by the same author and containing the complete, original text of the *De Antiquitate* with no later emendations. Where the *De Antiquitate* is characterized by numerous later editions, it appears from the extant original version of the *Gestis* that William of Malmesbury had also heard of inaccessible but credible archive documents in which the abbey's origins were clearly set in the time of the apostles or shortly after. Like a researcher wishing to use only those sources that he has checked himself, William does not dismiss this possibility, but he regards it as irrelevant in the absence of material proof. For us it is of course disquieting and frustrating to think that there might once have been other documents – kept elsewhere and since lost – with respect to this Joseph of Arimathaea. Such documents would not need to confirm his arrival at Glastonbury (which de Boron does not do either); it would be interesting and, for our purposes, enough for them to confirm the existence of some sort of Arimathaea tradition at Glastonbury reaching back, naturally, a long way before 1125. Meanwhile, it is indisputable that

*And by the bare tree is betokened
the world which is naked and
without fruit*

Right so alit a cloud betwixt them in likeness of a fire and a marvellous flame, that both their two shields burnt.

Malmesbury clearly kept this possibility open.

No one can prove that the monks asked William to maintain a certain discretion. On the other hand, it is difficult to escape the impression that Christianity at the time had a number of esoteric aspects, known only to insiders, as well as certain secrets whose point today escapes us. In any case, I am inclined to Geoffrey Ashe's view that it is more reasonable to assume that some very strange ideas existed in ancient Glastonbury than it is to believe the contrived explanations of the whole thing being hurriedly set up after the appearance of the first Grail stories. Furthermore, the importance given to literature in these theories is at odds with the religious perspective in which this sort of monastic community in around 1200 must be viewed. It is this that makes me sceptical about the alleged provenance of the prose *Lancelot* from a French Cistercian monastery.

Since the *De Antiquitate* is assumed to have undergone extensive emendation in about 1250, particularly in connection with King Arthur, it might be better just to disregard it. To do this, however, would mean overlooking the fact that the link between, on the one hand, Arthur and, on the other hand, Glastonbury and Gildas had already been made early on in the twelfth century in the *Vita Gildae* by Caradoc of Llancarfan, so that the emendator was not just making wild guesses. If this is admitted, it seems equally reasonable to envisage the possibility of the 'corrector' in 1240 referring to a source which enabled him to feel justified in making a similar link between Arimathaea and the abbey. In 1182, Chrétien de Troyes appears to have been ignorant of Joseph, so that the monks' tradition can hardly be derived from him. Shortly before 1200, de Boron got hold of part of the story, presumably during a stay in England. Apparently finding it a bit far-fetched for Joseph of Arimathaea to go to Glastonbury in person, he leaves him peacefully in Judaea while Bron and Alain bring the Grail to Britain in the company of Arimathaea's son Josephes, which does not make things any simpler.

It is interesting that this particular problem is more than an academic question, and is relevant, also, to the folklore of Somerset and Cornwall. With no thought for documentary reliability, the ordinary people have here allowed dreams to merge with reality. This sometimes leads to results that appear to bring us face to face with a different, often profounder reality. In this way, the folklore gives the impression of revealing the earliest origins of the mystery.

It all goes back to the fact, recorded by ancient writers like Pytheas (fourth century BC), Polybius (160 BC) and Diodorus Siculus (50 BC) and confirmed by archaeology, of the ancient export of tin, but also copper, lead and silver from Cornwall and the surrounding area to the lands around the Mediterranean Sea. Merchants of Semitic origin were involved in this. It is remarkable that in Cornish folk-tales, like *The Tinner of Chyannor*, those who managed the tin mines are described as beneficent Jews endowed with magic powers – surely an uncommon picture in the Christian world. Equally unusual is Polwhele's reference in 1803 in his *History of Cornwall* to the fact that, at that time, the oldest smelteries there were still called 'Jews' houses' and that the element jew frequently occurred in compound words connected with tin mining and the tin trade. Although the old industry and trade will have rested largely on the Phoenicians, who

*So Sir Bors departed from him
and rode the next way to the sea.
And at the last by fortune he
came to an Abbey which was*

And at the night they came unto a castle in a valley, closed with a running water, and with strong walls and high . . .

of course were also Semites, it would be wrong to disregard the possibility of a Jewish part in it. It is also recorded that tin-working artisans, such as the makers of organ pipes, would offer up a little prayer at the start of any delicate work, running: 'Joseph was in the trade.'

In the folklore of southwest England, then, Joseph of Arimathaea would be one of those who came regularly with their ships from, presumably, Tyre to Ictis, the bay round the impressive St Michael's Mount, near Marazion. According to an eastern tradition easily accepted in Cornwall, he was Mary's uncle and therefore the great-uncle of Jesus, 'who, as a young man, accompanied him to Britain'. From Marazion they would have started inland on foot or by horse, unless they first cleared Land's End to sail up to the mouth of the Brue. The journey is recalled in a number of place-names (Jesus' Well, Paradise, etc.). They are said to have stayed in Priddy, Somerset, in the old mining district of the Mendips, buying lead, copper and silver. After a trip through Cornwall, negotiating the purchase of tin, they then went to Ynis-Witrin, where Joseph had trading contacts among the inhabitants of the villages built on piles in the lake. These were close to the holy precinct of the later Glastonbury or Avalon, where the young Jesus, intelligent, curious by nature and interested in everything that people do, could talk to the druids. In Ynis-Witrin, the carpenter's son is supposed to have built the famous mud-walled church with His own hands. This, however, seems such a premature undertaking that one might wonder whether the hut was rather intended as a temporary lodging for the two of them.

Back home in Palestine after one of these trips, Jesus began His preaching. When it was all over, Joseph and a number of relatives and friends, possibly even with Mary among them, returned to the safety of Ynis-Witrin. Close to Wearyall Hill there used to be a quay, the existence of which is confirmed by archaeology, where they landed and Joseph planted his staff in the earth. This was immediately transformed into a thorn tree with branches, leaves and flowers. Up to the present day there have been descendants of this thorn growing in and around Glastonbury and flowering at Christmas according to the old calendar, modernized in 1752. Their Linnaean name is *crataegus oxyacantha praecox* and they stem, curiously enough, from the Near East. The travellers, finally, are said to have settled by the mud-walled 'church' and a local chieftain, Arviragus, gave them a large tract of farmland, though he refused to be converted.

And so they departed from the castle till they came to the seaside; and there they found the ship where Bors and Percivale were in, the which cried on the ship's board: Sir Galahad, ye be welcome, we have abiden you long.

7. THE MYSTERY OF THE GRAIL

And so the wind arose, and drove them through the sea in a marvellous pace.

Joseph of Arimathaea is said to have brought the Grail with him and this was immediately hidden, according to some, in Chalice Well. It is now time to leave the folklore in which, speedily followed by works of literature, Joseph is *not* left behind when the small group of early Christians moved to Avalon, but is clearly the leader of the expedition, and to return to the unemended William of Malmesbury. Here, there is a lengthy description of the floor of the little church, reputedly built by Jesus with His own hands, and long preserved by the use of artificial means, one of which was a lead covering. He quietly, almost provocatively quietly, adds: 'I think there here a holy mystery lies hidden.' It is a lapidary and highly frustrating pronouncement. Was he referring to the Grail while keeping the secret? Was he intrigued by certain astrological symbols in the floor paving?

Whoever visits All Souls' Church in the neighbouring Langport in Somerset will be able to make out an old stained-glass window (fifteenth century) showing Joseph of Arimathaea. In his hands he holds two pitchers, which, according to the *official* version, contain the sweat and the blood of Jesus. The story of the pitchers was recorded in the fourteenth century by a monk, John of Glastonbury. In his odd *Chronicle*, they are first mentioned as being found in the – from the point of view of

authenticity, extremely doubtful – *Prophecies of Melkin* (or Maelgwn), supposedly a fifth-century bard, who was proud to be a party to the story of Joseph's coming to Britain. Unfortunately, this figure is probably a figment of brother John's imagination. Of the Grail there is not a word, from him or from Melkin. If the abbey had been inclined to lift the story of the Grail from de Boron's book, this could only have been as a publicity stunt. There would in the circumstances have been no point in keeping it secret; quite the reverse, one would expect.

I therefore propose the following. For centuries, long before de Boron's or any other Arthurian romances were thought of, the monks of Glastonbury considered themselves the guardians of the Grail, i.e., the vessel with Christ's blood. They kept this secret, which corresponds to the idea expressed by Chrétien, that the Grail might only be discussed in special circumstances and by certain qualified persons. Since the relic was considered to be unimaginably holy the monks did not want to publicize their possession of it even though they knew that it was a source of enormous power for good. The reckless or perhaps inopportune revelation of the Grail would have led to the loss of its powers, which is a clearly magical train of thought. The secret would in time, however, leak out, as is evinced by the appearance of literary works like

*By then the ship went from the
land of Logris, and by adventure
it arrived up betwixt two rocks
passing great and
marvellous . . .*

*For sithen increased neither corn,
nor grass, nor well-nigh no fruit,
nor in the water was no fish;
wherefore men call it the lands of
the two marches, the waste land,
for that dolorous stroke.*

de Boron's *Joseph d'Arimathie*, Chrétien's eventually completed *Conte del Graal*, Wolfram von Eschenbach's *Parzival* and the anonymous *Perlesvaus*, whose author seems to know the countryside around Glastonbury. This writer not only sums up a number of recognizable features of the landscape, but also adds at the end of the work that he had found the story material in a holy monastery on the Isle of Avalon, 'at the edge of the Adventurous Marshes, where King Arthur and Queen Guinevere are laid to rest, according to the witness of God's servants who live there and know the whole story'.

Instead of regarding such books as a means of gaining publicity, as some literary historians believe, the abbey tried to safeguard its secret. Possibly because it was too good a story to be suppressed completely, it was reduced to innocent, less striking proportions. Instead of the Grail, Joseph's two pitchers appeared. These were more in line with the numerous stories then in circulation about the Holy Blood that had been brought to Europe from some crusade or other and which is still reverenced, among other places, at Bruges. Meanwhile, it is not impossible that from the abbey itself, but then in strict secrecy, the tradition of the Grail story should have been fostered among a circle of intellectually qualified adepts, almost like a sort of freemasonry (this was the great cathedral-building period in England too).

I consider such paradoxes to be in no way excluded in the later Middle Ages. We can even wonder if this was not a case of real leaks in the current sense of the word. Perhaps the Glastonbury clerics released certain information bit by bit, so as (a different view from those hitherto put forward) to secretly encourage the

Grail literature, without having started it themselves. De Boron mentions a 'big book' from an English monastery as his source of information, which was taken seriously by such a hyper-orthodox literary historian as R. S. Loomis; although we can of course wonder if the Burgundian poet was not simply referring to a copy of the Apocryphal *Gospel of Nicodemus*, which he may have found in Glastonbury.

Although R. S. Loomis was at the forefront of a school of literary historians whose members tend to greet any mention of Glastonbury in connection with the Grail tradition with nervous and animated dismissal, he himself considered seriously the possibility of a mysterious book that once belonged in the abbey library. For Loomis, this is a great concession, without, strangely enough, any particularly obvious reason. And yet there is a valid, albeit indirect, indication that certain secrets had been kept there.

The moment has now come to make a leap into the sixteenth century and to pay some attention to the figure of John Dee (1527–1608), one of the great minds of the age. He studied at Cambridge, Paris and Louvain, where he perfected his studies of geography under Mercator. Particularly adept at making navigational instruments, he was a great mathematician who propagated Euclidean geometry and its practical applications in England. Like Newton, he cherished an interest in alchemy and astrology and revealed himself as a forerunner of modern research into parapsychology, which in those days was anything but a discreditable activity for a scholar. In 1580 he suddenly went to Glastonbury, where he hoped to unravel certain secrets in the art of alchemy but where he largely spent his time investigating a strange phenomenon that he

And there he dwelled an eight days, and at the ninth day there fell a great wind which departed him out of the isle, and brought him to another isle by a rock . . .

Is that sooth? said he. Now by my head, said he, ye be ill arrayed; and then turned he again unto the cliff fortress.

apparently knew about before his arrival there. According to him, there is in this region, which he refers to in the Welsh fashion of the Arthur romances as the *Kingdom of Logres*, an enormous zodiac spread out over the landscape. He made notes on this, which are still extant, and drew in a number of zodiacal figures on a map. The interest shown in this zodiac by John Dee, who was also counsellor to Queen Elizabeth I, was possibly connected with his practice of alchemy. I am thinking, for example, of the *Emerald Tables* of Hermes Trismegistus, pointing out the correspondence between the structure of the macrocosm and that of the microcosm. Certain aspects of this correlation between alchemy and astrology can also be detected in Wolfram's *Parzival*. Were there traces of this in the church floor that intrigued William of Malmesbury?

In apparently complete ignorance of John Dee (and she would certainly have used the reference had she known it), the artist and sculptor Kathleen Maltwood arrived at the same conclusion as him in 1925, on the basis of a study of *Perlesvaus*, which she was going to illustrate, and with the help of the local Ordnance Survey Map. She found confirmation for her view in a series of excellent aerial photographs that she commissioned, which are now on show in the office of the Chalice Well Trust, and published, unfortunately not particularly brilliant books on the subject. The Glastonbury Zodiac, rediscovered by her and originating by her calculations in 3000 BC, is 10 miles in diameter and is formed by hills, streams, rivers, ancient roads and pathways, fields, woods and other natural topographical features, as well as by a number of deliberate human alterations in the

face of the landscape. From ground level, hardly anything of this can be seen, not even from the top of the Tor, but one is inclined, after seeing the aerial photographs and the outlines superimposed on the map, to give Kathleen Maltwood's discovery a chance, albeit cautiously. According to her, the Zodiac's constellations correspond to figures and animals encountered by the heroes of *Perlesvaus* at the appropriate points in their quest, which would point to a very ancient initiation rite. It is remarkable in this respect that in the prose *Lancelot*, Perceval's aunt recounts that the Round Table was made by Merlin and is particularly important since it represents the vault of the heavens with the stars and planets. This can hardly refer to a mundane piece of furniture, and so we look it up in *Perlesvaus* and discover there that the Round Table could feed 1000 people and 150 bulls. This ecological reference can clearly be used to imply that this was a whole district with a special astrological or astronomical significance.

With the idea in our minds that nothing is too crazy to be included in the Arthurian tradition, we might be inclined to disregard both Maltwood's theories and the alleged literary evidence of the Grail stories. This would, however, be an overhasty reaction. We are still left with John Dee's notes. Of course, he might be wrong as well, but where on earth did he get the idea from? In the present context it is almost totally irrelevant to wonder whether the thing itself is real or fictitious. John Dee was a serious researcher. He would certainly not have undertaken the trip to far-off Glastonbury if he had not discovered the existence of an acknowledged secret tradition, presumably newly accessible as a result of the dissolution of the

And when they heard these words they fell down to the earth and were astonied; and therewith

As soon as ye three come to the City of Sarras, there to achieve the Holy Grail, ye shall find me under a tower arrived . . .

abbey. He need not even have been motivated by occult considerations. It may have been the almost unimaginable surveying achievement that attracted him as an instrument maker, mathematician and specialist in Euclidean geometry.

Meanwhile, no one, as far as I am concerned, need believe the story of the Glastonbury Zodiac. The important point is that this is probably the tip of the iceberg. By this I mean that the abbey may have guarded these or similar, possibly wholly imaginary, secrets. It is enough that there should be one such secret for there to be the possibility of several. Here, for the first time, we have reasonable proof of the existence of something resembling an esoteric current involving the Grail and with astrological implications. Alongside this, it is relatively unimportant whether or not John Dee hoped to find the secret of the philosophers' stone in Glastonbury.

It was inevitable that the Grail should lose its hermetic character after a time and become an exoteric symbol. After the dissolution of their house in 1539, a number of the Glastonbury monks fled to Wales. There they took refuge in the sister foundation at Strata Florida in Cardiganshire, not yet hit by the draconian measures of Henry VIII. Rightly fearing that this new spiritual shelter was about to fall victim to the persecution of the monasteries, one of them passed on to the local noble family Powell of Nanteos a simple wooden drinking bowl, which, according to an existing tradition, had already been regarded as the Grail before it left Glastonbury. It is a poor, dilapidated thing, credited with healing powers if water is drunk from it. It seems, by its movingly poor

appearance, much more credible as the vessel used by Jesus at the Last Supper than the gem-encrusted, dressed-up chalices that we know from literary iconography. In 1855, Richard Wagner went specially to Wales to see this simple drinking bowl. That was seven years after he had written *Lohengrin*, and long before he wrote his – albeit already contemplated – *Parsifal*.

So, according to de Boron, the Grail had arrived in Avalon-Glastonbury. This particular branch of the saga could now develop and grow towards the Arthurian world. Because of man's sinfulness, the Grail was brought for protection to a castle, called Corbenic or Munsalvaesche and identified by some with Monségur (Languedoc) or by others with the Welsh fortress of Dinas Bran (Denbighshire). Distances in space seem to play no part here, which corresponds to the strange nature of the geographical locations in the stories of the Round Table. There is also a strong impression that in the Grail castle there is no – or at least there is another – dimension of time. The castle is situated preferably on a high mountaintop, somewhere by a river, a lake or the sea. Islands, too, seem suitable places. In this respect, it belongs to the ancient Celtic otherworld and, therefore, to the kingdom of the dead. This is in line with its not completely inaccessible character as regards earthly mortals such as Arthur's knights. Since it can come and go like a *fata morgana* (the expression is derived from the Italian versions of the Round Table romances), and the way to it is repeatedly lost, as many find to their cost, it remains difficult – if not impossible – to reach and enter, as we know from Wagner's *Lohengrin*. A magician like Merlin, on the other hand, knows more about it: disguised as a woodcutter, he can direct the lost Perceval to

*So the wind arose, and drove the
barge from the land, and all
knights beheld it till it was out of
their sight.*

117

Forthwith there fell a sudden tempest and a thunder, lightning, and rain, as all the earth would have broken.

the pathway that leads to it. The regions between Camelot and Corbenic-Munsalvaesche sometimes appear to be filled with horrible dangers. It seems a sort of twilight zone, a fracture in space and time, belonging to a strange dimension where the roving adventurer is threatened by events beyond the conventional laws of nature.

We know little of how the interior of the Grail castle was supposed to look. We are, however, left with the impression that it is tinged with an eastern splendour as pictured by medieval man in the period of the Crusades. This is the dwelling of the keeper of the Grail, the ailing Fisher-King, with his glittering court, often including enchanting and, despite the sanctified nature of the castle, not even so very coy women, strongly reminiscent of fairies and undoubtedly denizens of the otherworld. One of these will give herself to Gawain and become the mother of Galahad. This is all clearly characteristic of Avalon and Ynis-Witrin: in short, of the Celtic idea of the afterlife. Perhaps stranger still is the fact that in Wolfram von Eschenbach the Grail is worshipped and protected by a group of knights that as good as constitutes a separate religious order. He calls them by an undeniably very confusing name: they are designated as *Templeisen*, or Templars, the same as the members of the military religious order founded by French knights and reaching its apogee at about this time, before being finally destroyed by the pope and King Philippe IV in 1311 on a charge of heresy and the practice of magic. Did the Templars indeed adhere to an esoteric, perhaps magical doctrine and was the Bavarian poet aware of this?

Perhaps the Grail had to be so well guarded

because, as Albrecht von Scharfenberg has it in *Der jüngere Titurel* (1270), it could float invisibly in the air. Expressed in current terms, this would mean that it could move into another dimension and then materialize again in the three-dimensional world. This phenomenon probably explains the rumbling thunderclap with which it sometimes appears, accompanied by fragrant perfumes and covered by a white silken cloth, before the knights of the Round Table at King Arthur's court, to the wonder and amazement of everyone present. Thanks to the Grail, they are provided with wonderful meals, though nothing indicates that it is filled with victuals. Manifestly imbued with magical powers, it heals the sick and even, in Lancelot's case, someone rendered insane by unrequited love. It also heals the deepest wounds; only the ailing Fisher-King cannot, apparently, be helped by the Grail, at least not without questions that are at the same time spontaneous and ritually formulated, though it does prolong his existence. This it does for all those living within range of its power. Whoever has beheld the Grail cannot suffer death for the week following.

In its purely Christian form, the Grail appears finally as a chalice during the offertory, out of which the child Jesus or the naked, crucified God rises up. This illustrates rather bewilderingly a theological view which occupied people's minds at the time, namely the corporeal presence of Christ during the Eucharist. It is exactly contemporaneous with the fourth Lateran Council's promulgation of the dogma of transubstantiation (1215), quickly followed by the subsequent miracles. In 1254, the town of Douai in northeastern France was graced with the miraculous appearance of Christ's image on a

And then he lift up his hand and blessed him, and so took his arms and made him ready; and so by adventure he came by a strand, and found a ship the which was without sail or oar.

And he answered and saluted him again, and asked him: What is your name? for much my heart giveth unto you. Truly, said he, my name is Launcelot du Lake. Sir, said he, then be ye welcome, for ye were the beginner of me in this world. Ah, said he, are ye Galahad?

host in the chalice, first as a baby and later as the Man of Sorrows, as recorded by Thomas of Cantimpré. This is a sign of God's grace, which man can reach via the Grail and which amounts to a part of Paradise. The two would later coalesce into one in Gert van der Schuren's *Kroniek van Kleef* (1478). There, the Knight of the Swan appears, introduced in Antwerp as Parzival's son Lohengrin and already presaged by those who completed Chrétien's unfinished work. Of him it is said that he came from Paradise, which ordinary people also call the Grail.

Corbenic and its inhabitants clearly belong to a parallel world, as is shown by its symmetrical and complementary juxtaposition to Camelot with its court of King Arthur and the Round Table, which is also meant to receive the Grail. Corbenic and Camelot relate to each other like the communicating vessels in physics. With a hierarchical emphasis on the Grail castle, they are both esoteric centres linked by a magical two-way traffic. When the knights of the Round Table, which in its form is an archetypal symbol of creation and perfection, set out on a quest, they are continuously confronted with obstacles or are drawn into all sorts of time-consuming, often mortally dangerous exploits. It reminds us in some ways of modern science fiction. Meanwhile, the aim of the quest is always to behold the Grail, for them the most valuable object on earth.

In connection with the relationship between Camelot and Corbenic, the poets apparently nowhere hit on Plato's dual world picture. It nonetheless embodies a general human, and, therefore, archetypal pattern in which reality and hyper-reality coexist and possibly overlap. These are not hermetically separated from each other

and they influence one another. Arthur has no magic powers and lives in the mundane, three-dimensional reality, like a more earthly reflection of the Fisher-King, who exists in a timeless, higher space and just cannot die. Under the influence of this situation, the picture of Arthur gradually changes. From a fearless warrior, he evolves into a rather detached, withdrawn father-figure who appears to accept the idea of Guinevere's continually deceiving him with Lancelot, still his bosom friend. Imbued with the idea of the Grail, he lives for an unspecified higher purpose and has even to be goaded by Guinevere into taking up his sword again and setting out on a quest himself.

Chrétien's own original part of the *Conte del Graal* could be described as the seminal *Perceval*. There is nothing to indicate here that the poet regards the Grail, which to him is a mysterious talisman, as ever having received Christ's blood. No one knows how he was intending to develop the story further when it was cut short by his death. Under the influence of Robert de Boron and of the *Lancelot* compilation, the Grail quickly became a chalice or, in some cases, a ciborium. There can, in any case, be no doubt but that it stems from a prehistoric symbol. We can imagine that the monks in Glastonbury Abbey realized this and precisely for this reason kept so very quiet about an artifact from pagan times that they had, perhaps, unearthed by accident. One of the handsomest objects from the peat layers of the Ynis-Witrin lakes is a bronze dish known as the Glastonbury Bowl and preserved in Taunton Museum. This may have been preceded by other, similar finds in the early Middle Ages, but the bowl itself evokes spontaneous Grail associations in the public imagination, without any need for

Often they arrived in isles far
from folk, where there repaired
none but wild beasts . . .

So it befell on a night, at midnight, he arrived afore a castle, on the back side, which was rich and fair, and there was a postern opened toward the sea, and was open without any keeping . . .

specific commentary in that direction.

Research into the origin of the Grail usually involves the assumption that this ought to be found in the Celtic tradition. Its prehistoric form is assumed to correspond to a cauldron or dish that plays an important part in mythology, namely the Vessel of Plenty. The provision of celebratory feasts was a popular custom with the Celts, naturally respected in the otherworld too, where the dead heroes whiled away eternity in feasting with the gods. Such vessels could not be missed in that other land of the living, since they possessed the magic power of providing unlimited quantities of the most delicious foods and drinks. We are reminded of certain fairy-tale motifs like the Land of Cockaigne. As a precursor of the Grail, the Vessel of Plenty also had the power of raising the dead. In the earliest recorded Welsh folk-tales, such as *Culhwch and Olwen* and *The Plundering of Annwn*, just such vessels are the goal of adventurous raids in which Arthur, too, participates and which look forward from their rougher form to the later quests of the knights of the Round Table. There is also a poisonous spear, by which the god Bran is wounded in the foot and so killed. This has led to the identification of Bran as the original figure for the ailing Fisher-King, suffering from an incurable wound, as well as with de Boron's Hebron or Bron. Whether or not the author was perhaps playing on his own name – Boron, Bron – is a question that no one has asked.

So many, and so many different, elements converge in the Grail saga that it is pointless to neglect the Vessel of Plenty and Bran's lance as two of the seeds from which it grew, particularly since they go a long way to explaining Arthur's relation to the Grail.

It is also true, however, that they signify just one step in a more comprehensive process of development. They are part of a broader, more general context, on which Professor Jessie Weston so penetratingly insisted in her virtually breathtaking study *From Ritual to Romance* (1919) and so, in my view, approached the heart of the matter. I have the impression, however, that her theories have received too little attention. This is presumably the result of the very limited emancipation of even academically prominent women at the time her book appeared. It is certainly principally connected with the fact that a lot of research has been exclusively directed to the old Celtic origins and is still being so directed, with very little further evidence being given of any imagination.

Jessie Weston's basic assumption is that in researching the mystery of the Grail the figure of the ailing Fisher-King must be regarded as central. Then there is the hero – Perceval, Galahad and also Gawain – who is expected to ask a specific question with respect to the Grail and the bleeding lance. If he does this accurately, the king will be healed and his country, which lies barren and waste all around, will be restored to its old prosperity. This is the precise point of departure, although it seldom appears as precisely as this and the strangest variants may be encountered. This gives the impression that the medieval poets did not generally understand what they were about. Some authors go so far as to turn the whole thing round, as it were. They introduce a perfectly healthy king with a flourishing country, who falls ill and sees his lands ruined only when the expected, but in the circumstances meaningless, question is not asked. This is apparently a completely erroneous

So Sir Launcelot departed, and took his arms, and said he would go see the realm of Logris, which I have not seen these twelve months.

123

And on the morn he turned unto Camelot, where he found King Arthur and the Queen. But many of the knights of the Round Table were slain and destroyed, more than half.

interpretation of an ancient story, which is faithfully reproduced only in some exceptional texts, such as the *Sone de Nansai* (before 1250) from the French Brabant. Otherwise only Chrétien in 1182 still seems to know exactly what it was about.

A similar seminal element is used to illustrate the theory developed by the anthropologist Sir James G. Frazer (1854–1941) in his standard work *The Golden Bough*. This comes down to the fact that in so-called primitive communities the fertility of the land, including its inhabitants and its animals, was regarded as dependent on the physical well-being of the chieftain or king. This concept is the earthly reflection of the mythical ideas held by the community concerned. In this context Jessie Weston points to the Near East, where the once related fertility gods like Attis, Tammuz and Mithras, apparently not without some influences from ancient India, gave shape to the eternal natural cycle of death and rebirth. She traces the Attis belief to some of the Gnostic sects that, in the melting-pot of the early church, held such fertility lore of de- and regeneration to be in no way in contradiction to the remembrance of the crucified and resurrected Son of God, though this link was later to be suppressed by the official church or, rather, tacitly adopted. Jessie Weston, however, takes into account the possibility of a comparable *gnosis* (the word means knowledge) reaching the west, and more particularly the Celtic world, in the first centuries of the Christian era. She sees this as happening in the specific form of Mithraism, imported by the Roman legions. This religion is known to have lasted in particularly isolated areas, such as the Swiss mountains and the Vosges, until the fifth century. Traces of it are thought to exist in the

sword dances and Morris dances still practised in Britain and elsewhere.

Jessie Weston also devotes particular attention to the so-called mumming plays, or masques. These are based on texts that have been handed down from generation to generation. The plays are a sort of rudimentary popular theatre that is performed in the streets at Christmas or Easter to everyone's great enjoyment. The characters, armed with sticks or wooden swords, move in the same direction as the sun. The otherwise generally incoherent plot always involves a struggle between a negative, demonic figure and a trapped, naturally positive hero. There is sometimes also a dragon, as well as a rider on an imitation horse, the so-called hobby-horse. In the clearly recognizable struggle representing nature's decline and reawakening, there is at first sight a less obvious link between this pantomime horse and the prehistoric fertility goddess, who in certain circumstances was represented as a mare. The hero, consistently called St George, does in fact die, but he is always brought back from the dead by the doctor, apparently originally an all-powerful magician or perhaps a druid. Just as in the folk dances mentioned above, the mumming plays are about the struggle between the fertility of the summer and the barrenness of winter. Apart from that, the doctor inevitably reminds one of the *dottore* from the Italian *commedia dell'arte*, an artistically more polished genre, but apparently derived from similar, though distant, sources.

Jessie Weston is right to consider these mumming plays, about the fertility of crops and animals and the triumphant struggle of light against darkness, as a leftover from prehistoric nature rites. This view leads to the conclusion

*Then he came into a perilous
forest where he found the well the
which boileth with great
waves . . .*

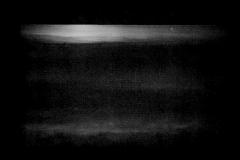

And a little afore even the sword arose great and marvellous, and was full of great heat that many men fell for dread.

that such rites later developed into folk-tales and that these eventually led to the Arthurian and Grail epics. I think the Grail may in this case be associated with the box in which the players collect their money from the public or with the medicines administered by the doctor. In any case, King Arthur sometimes appears in the mumming, while we can wonder if, in the cases where Arthur does not appear, the figure of Father Christmas, who likewise appears, should not be identified with him.

It is clear that the dying and reviving hero corresponds in certain respects to the ailing, virtually condemned king. While Jessie Weston seems to be mainly interested in this correspondence, she also looks into the origins of the figure of the doctor. In the Arthurian romances she finds only one character that, albeit fairly inconspicuously, has the necessary talent for, or interest in, healing, namely Sir Gawain, Gauvain or Walewein, and this particularly in the Flemish *Lancelot* (1326). She interprets this as indicating that he, though later supplanted by Perceval and Galahad, was originally the main character in the Grail epic. He in fact knew the innermost secrets of the Grail and understood how to cure the ailing monarch, so lifting the curse that lay on his land.

Like some Agatha Christie of literary history, Jessie Weston picks up this one thread and carefully follows it through. She had noticed that the pseudo-Wauchier's continuation of Chrétien's *Perceval* explicitly and repeatedly claims to derive its information about Gauvain from a story by Bleheris that the count of Poitiers had originally been very taken with. I have already drawn attention to repeated mention of this nonetheless very mysterious figure, who was

even to end up as one of the *dramatis personae* of the Grail epic. From the frequent references to this Bleheris, Bleris or whatever other variants may occur, Jessie Weston concludes that none other than he himself (he also appears in Germany as early as Eilhart von Oberge's *Tristan* in 1170) first added the mystery of the Grail to the already existing Arthurian material. This might have been done in a veiled way, which would then not have been fully understood by his successors.

Without assuming that he was necessarily an adept, Professor Weston suggests the possibility that Bleris knew of the existence and nature of esoteric communities practising, if not Mithraism, then a secret cult derived from it, within a strictly closed circle whose initiation rites could have included a simulated but terrifying confrontation with death and the hereafter. Cumont, the great specialist on the subject, does in fact mention that Mithraism penetrated as far as Wales in the Roman period. The cult we are here concerned with would understandably be a highly secret *gnosis*, as seems to be confirmed by the fact that the *Elucidation* later added at the beginning of Chrétien's text has Bleris himself underline how serious the subject is and what the fateful consequences will be for whoever might reveal the secret. Possibly Chrétien himself did not appreciate how explosive the subject was that he was dealing with, though those who completed his book, on the other hand, sometimes appear to do so. This explains why the Damsel with the White Mule insistently informs Perceval that she will not answer even if he should ask her 100 times for the secret. Furthermore, whoever learns it starts trembling and looks appalling, gripped by an indescribable terror. It does not

*So it befell him in good
adventure he came into the realm
of Logris . . .*

So after the quest of the Sangreal was fulfilled, and all knights that were left a-live were come again unto the Table Round, as the book of the Sangreal maketh mention, then was there great joy in the court . . .

take much effort to imagine that the Grail is no more than a ritual bowl or goblet, but that its great secret is hidden in the missing background information: the role it shares with the lance as a polarizer of the magic powers that govern life and death.

On the basis of the anthropological ideas of her time, Professor Weston looked closer at the relation between Attis, Adonis and Tammuz. Looking further back in time, she sought the origin of their cults in the ancient civilizations of the Indus. Finally, she found strongly similar elements in Mithraism with respect to the eternal cycle of life and death. Mithraism originated in Persia but became popular enough to reach the west, via Rome and its legions, almost 2000 years ago. With the simultaneous, energetic and virtually parallel spread of Christianity, it was lost to view. According to Jessie Weston, it nonetheless survived in smaller, closed communities as a secret, persistent and possibly wildly variegated doctrine up as far as the early Middle Ages. It is here that the roots of the first Grail stories would have originated, known to Bleris and possibly other initiates, whence they later came to be merged with the Arthurian legends.

Because of its wider view, this theory is more attractive than the still fashionable concept of a purely Celtic, or even largely Irish, derivation that was fairly suddenly transplated to France.

Jessie Weston's hypothesis of a fertility cult known on the Continent, or made known, through Bleris' tales and then integrated in the Arthurian stories deserves to be viewed as a brilliant discovery. It ties in with an archetypal substrate that is much broader than that of any analysis based exclusively on the lances of Bran or Lug, vessels of plenty and other paraphernalia of the Celtic gods and heroes. It can possibly be objected that the survival of a Mithraic ritual via a centuries-old succession of initiates right up to the Grail romances of 1200 would mean passing through the very narrow neck of a sandglass. The cauldron of plenty or the bloodied lance in comparison to this are no more, however, than fragmentary elements, local trimmings that can, on the other hand, be meaningfully incorporated in the mythical structure proposed by Jessie Weston.

Furthermore, she sees the whole thing in a particularly broad perspective, going from the Indian Rig-Veda, via the Sumerian Tammuz, to the Persian Mithras, who then finally reaches the Atlantic Ocean together with the Roman armies, which, anthropologically, amounts to a so-called migration phenomenon. Since she herself built on the theories in Frazer's *The Golden Bough*, we are obliged to consider what Chesterton in the *Ballad of the White Horse* intuitively and sharply called 'the gods before the gods'. We may suppose that fertility rites were part of the very early pattern of human religious behaviour, wherever people were, further away even than ancient India or Persia, but also much closer. The English mumming plays referred to by Weston may possibly be connected with Mithraic ritual, so eroded by the passing years as to be unrecognizable. We can, however, distinguish much older remnants in a similar but even more strongly disorientating ceremony that is not mentioned by her. This is the Horn Dance, which is still performed every September at Abbots Bromley in Staffordshire. In this, six dancers appear in deer antlers, the deer men, challenging each other with the horns and being hunted by an

So when Sir Launcelot was
departed, the queen outward
made no manner of sorrow in
showing to none of his blood nor
to none other.

And thus it passed on until the morn, and the king and the queen and all manner of knights that were there at that time drew them unto the meadow beside Westminster where the battle should be.

archer. The dance is considered to be a survival from the Ice Age hunters in northwestern Europe, intended to increase the herds and to ensure the success of the hunt. After the show, local farmers still appreciate a visit from the deer men, which is regarded as good for the crops and livestock. What we have here is clearly the echo of a prehistoric fertility ritual, such as can be seen in the cave paintings of Lascaux in the Dordogne in France and elsewhere, which takes us back 20,000 years into the past without – and this is the point – us having to accompany Jessie Weston to India.

In the scattered living folklore of western Europe there are therefore traces of very ancient ritual. When we look closely at the mumming plays, these definitely show a certain resemblance to the situation depicted in the medieval romances. A powerful, patently symbolic figure is ill, dying or already dead, which is directly connected with the coming of winter and with the barrenness and other plagues with which his lands are afflicted. He has at his disposal a number of magical objects, which can, however, only be effectively used when a hero appears who asks precisely the required ritual question. This is expected to heal or revive the king, restoring as well the prosperity of the country. This is a pattern that lends expression to far-off, ancestral fertility customs. These need not have been imported from the east, in spite of the commonplace *ex oriente lux*, since they are also part and parcel of how westerners since the last Ice Age have pictured the mystery and the rhythm of nature.

So this passed on all that winter,
with all manner of hunting and
hawking, and jousts and
tourneys were many betwixt
many great lords . . .

8.   ARTHUR THE GOD

Strange to relate, Weston does not mention that in 1911 Frazer himself had already referred in *The Golden Bough* to a passage from *Perlesvaus* in order to illustrate one of his basic points. The passage relates how Lancelot is met by a cheering population and offered the crown, in place of the recently dead king. The knight soon learns that on the old king's death the capital city caught fire and that the flames cannot be put out until a worthy successor is found. Furthermore, the coronation must take place on New Year's Day in the middle of the fire. This unusual procedure for the succession naturally signifies the immediate death by burning of the new monarch, at which point Lancelot gracefully declines. Accompanied by one of the most beautiful ladies of the country, a dwarf then appears on the scene who is prepared to change places with Lancelot, who then hurriedly takes to his heels. In typically naïve style, and with no indication of the true nature of the incident, however clear it might appear to us, the writer then adds: 'The ladies and damsels said that he did not want to be king because death did not attract him.'

In fact, Frazer could have found many better examples in the Grail literature. I mention it here only to show that he himself considered it a link with the Arthurian world. The death of a monarch sets his capital on fire and this can be extinguished only after the coronation of a new

head of state. We are left with the impression that the thirteenth-century poet has completely lost the thread here because of his ignorance, or lack of comprehension, of the original facts. His reasoning seems to be that if Lancelot wants to save the town, there is no alternative but for him to be consumed by the flames during the coronation. To escape from this fatal circle, the writer appeals to something of which he is apparently vaguely aware; something that might be called an ancestral memory released by the subconscious and precisely for this reason true to tradition, but only incompletely comprehended. Hence the writer has the crown given to a deputy, which saves Lancelot's life but leaves the audience bewildered and abandoned, except perhaps for a feeling of sympathy for the poor old dwarf. It is one of the typical and disconcerting about-faces that make these stories so often opaque or even annoying for the reader, but which are clearly the result of the author's not understanding, or misinterpreting, the traditions. This sometimes leads to almost comical situations. In the same book, for example, there is the case of the Grail-bearing damsel who loses her hair because Perlesvaus fails to ask the relevant question.

To fully appreciate the example of Lancelot's adventure taken by Frazer from *Perlesvaus*, however absurd it might be in itself, we need to

And thus it passed on from Candlemass until after Easter, that the month of May was come, when every lusty heart beginneth to blossom, and to bring forth fruit; for like as herbs and trees bring forth fruit and flourish in May, in likewise every lusty heart that is in any manner a lover, springeth and flourisheth in lusty deeds.

*For like as winter rasure doth
alway arase and deface green
summer, so fareth it by unstable
love in man and woman.*

bear in mind certain aspects of the anthropologist's work. After a study of the behaviour patterns of innumerable peoples throughout the world, he arrived at the following conclusion.

In real life among certain communities still living in a state of nature, and more or less concealed in the mythological mists of more highly developed early civilizations, the custom seems to exist of, at a given moment, putting a violent end to the life of the king, the human embodiment of the godhead. 'If I understand correctly,' writes Sir James Frazer, 'the motive for the murder of the human god is the fear that, owing to the undermining of the body by illness or old age, his god-like spirit should be subject to a corresponding decline, affecting the whole course of nature and the existence of his worshippers, who imagine the cosmic powers to be dependent on those of their human godhead.'

At an apparently inevitable stage in human and mythological evolution, the phenomenon therefore appears of the deified king's being eliminated because his failing powers are considered no longer capable of suffusing his surroundings with the necessary energy. On his death a new king is designated, thereby safeguarding for a time the hunting or agricultural community's dependence on nature. It is this sort of ancient custom that comes briefly to the surface, in a very confused way, in the passage quoted from *Perlesvaus* and which was recognized as such by Frazer.

The barbarian, if fairly simple, behaviour pattern of decline, sacrifice and succession of the old chieftain by the new does lead, however, to appreciably more complicated situations. In explicitly matriarchal communities, considered to

be the oldest existing ones, it would have been the custom for the king, who in fact was no more than a prince consort, to be killed each year and replaced by another. An echo of this is possibly to be found in Greek literature with the murder of the Mycenean Agamemnon, who, according to some interpretations, was killed by his wife Clytemnestra and her lover Aegisthus 'just' because his normal period as monarch had run out. This essentially catastrophic situation did not last. The monarch condemned to death by the sacred law soon began to escape his lot by the substitution of a descendant, prisoner-of-war or even a volunteer like the dwarf in *Perlesvaus*. Before being sacrificed to the gods, the substitute would enjoy all the kingly prerogatives, including access to the royal harem, for a time if only to keep up appearances.

This ancient blueprint seems today to be retained in the surprising context of the Carnival (Mardi Gras) and the election of a Carnival Prince. Frazer cites as an example the custom of the English village Lostwithiel in Cornwall, practised until the sixteenth century, of crowning a 'king' for a day and organizing a splendid banquet for him. The 'coronation' took place at Easter, at the beginning of the fertile spring, with the cooperation of the church and of the local authorities. The fertility ritual, lasting for hundreds of years, or for thousands of years in the case of customs like the above, or like masques and folk-dances, had long before the advent of Christianity been replaced by animal sacrifices, as was also true of Mithraism.

According to Jessie Weston, the presence in the Grail saga of the motif of the ailing king whose country lies wasting around him points to a survival of the prehistoric relation between the

For in many persons there is no stability; for we may see all day, for a little blast of winter's rasure, anon we shall deface and lay apart true love for little or nought, that cost much thing; this is no wisdom nor stability, but it is feebleness of nature and great disworship, whomsoever useth this.

But nowadays men can not love seven night but they must have all their desires: that love may not endure by reason; for where they be soon accorded, and hasty heat, soon it cooleth.

physical and mental condition of the community's demigod chief and the world of nature. Everything revolves round this basic situation. The tradition, however, took firm root at the point when a new insight took shape: not the king's death, but his health was important, so that his recovery would suffice. In this way a dialogue ritual evolved in which questions and answers were to play a fundamental role. Magically charged objects, powerful talismans connected with the maintenance and reproduction of life, came to be added: the feminine Grail and the masculine lance. The former, representing the vulva, presumably made the most spectacular impression and acquired precedence over possibly several cult objects. Meanwhile, it seems to me to be an acceptable notion that the dangerous and often absurd adventures of the Round Table knights in the literature – Round Table which itself amounts to a symbolic representation of the cosmos, which must be kept going by ritual practices – are the later reflection of forgotten initiation trials to which, originally, the successor and, later, the saviour-substitute of the dying or ailing king and his country had to submit.

The secret of the Grail appears therefore to be connected, and can even be identified, with an ancient fertility cult, almost as old as humanity itself, and possibly with the continued existence of the whole of creation. Stories of this may have reached Chrétien de Troyes, but it is not clear how he reacted to them. It must be remembered that he was unable to complete his *Conte del Graal*, so that a possible gradual revelation of the mystery remained in abeyance. It cannot, however, be excluded that he himself had insufficient information at his disposal. It is, on the other hand, difficult to deny that he knew something. Although he did not confuse the Grail with a chalice or a ciborium, he did regard the Grail as a holy object, borne, however, by a damsel and not by a man, i.e., not by a priest. What he knew did not necessarily come from Bleris, but, since Bleris appears earlier in Eilhart von Oberge's *Tristan* (1170), it is possible that he had some justifiable reason for not naming Bleris as having revealed traditional secrets, bearing in mind that the *Elucidation* is a later addition. Be that as it may, Bleris is mentioned as source or as protagonist only in what others, possibly less scrupulous about a tacit agreement with respect to secrecy, have added to Chrétien's unfinished text.

Apart from this, there is another possible explanation for the fact that the Grail story first appeared from Chrétien's pen. The prologue ends with the poet telling us that he is about to embark on the finest story ever told at a king's court. For this, he has a book at his disposal, presumably in prose, which Count Philippe of Flanders, also called Philippe of Alsace, has provided. The story will be called – in his spelling – *Li Contes del Graal*. This message consists of only seven lines of verse and yet it is made quite clear that the Grail that provides the title of the poem is considered by the author to be the pivot around which the rest revolves. The book that his patron handed on to him is highly intriguing. The direction mention of '*li quens Phelipes de Flandres*' (Count Philippe of Flanders), who, furthermore, maintained relations with England and was involved in the political struggle for the English crown, leaves the impression that Chrétien de Troyes did not invent this particular. It is difficult to imagine that he would run the risk

Therefore all ye that be lovers
call unto your remembrance the
month of May, like as did Queen
Guenever, for whom I make here

lived she was a true lover, and
therefore she had a good end.

And so upon the morn they took their horses with the queen, and rode a-Maying in woods and meadows as it pleased them, in great joy and delights; for the queen had cast to have been again with King Arthur at the furthest by ten of the clock, and so was that time her purpose.

of hearing his employer afterwards banteringly proclaiming that the whole thing was a fabrication.

What we have here is the steadfastly repeated and particularly persistent notion of one or more existing books, lost in the meantime, from which the authors of the Arthur cycle, and more particularly of the Grail contribution, appear to have taken their material. In this respect, it is worth noting that in 956–7 the abbot of Glastonbury, later canonized as Dunstan, who had had the level of the cemetery raised and possibly Arthur's grave marked by the lead cross, was staying in Ghent, where the counts of Flanders also had their residence at the time. He had come as a temporary political exile and had been welcomed by the widowed Countess Eltrudis, herself an English princess, and her son Baudouin II. They arranged for him to be lodged in St Peter's Abbey on Blandinus Hill, which was under their protection. Abbot Dunstan was one of the intellectuals, even scientists, of his day. Moreover, he was a passionate collector of manuscripts and himself a writer. In the chaotic context of the wars against the Danes, he had been obliged to counter an apparently substantial revival of paganism and superstition with a mainly Celtic bent. Since he had an enquiring mind and was not bigoted, he might have been extremely interested in various aspects of this phenomenon. It is possible that he was thus confronted with fertility customs that had probably never been completely eliminated. Did he pass his time in Ghent by writing down his experience of these? Or perhaps he was more concerned with traditions and secrets from his own beloved abbey? I am thinking of the story about Joseph of Arimathaea, or possibly a legend

about a magic object, perhaps well on the way to becoming the Christian Grail. Perhaps he wrote down the tales from Somerset and the surrounding area about King Arthur, whose grave he knew to be in Glastonbury since he himself had, with a view to keeping it secret, arranged for it to be covered by a new layer of topsoil. We can, in short, postulate the possibility that Dunstan left behind him in the abbey at Ghent a book that he had written, or perhaps a valuable manuscript that he, as a bibliophile, had brought with him. This, or possibly a copy of it, could later have come into the possession of the counts of Flanders and thence into the hands of Chrétien de Troyes.

This may be pure hypothesis, but I think it important to point out a clearly non-hypothetical connection between Glastonbury and Ghent, which prompted, furthermore, the conclusive adoption of the Cistercian rule at Glastonbury after Dunstan's rehabilitation and return to his abbey. Alongside this, it is remarkable that it should be Philippe's father, Diederik of Alsace, who is traditionally credited with bringing the Holy Blood to Bruges during the Crusades.

Meanwhile, I am not aware of whether anyone has ever seriously gone into the question of why the Grail knight Lohengrin should have been sent by Wolfram von Eschenbach in 1200 precisely to Antwerp, an unimportant town at the outer edge of the Empire which had scarcely begun its first stone defences.

Strangely enough, Antwerp had less than a century before been the scene of the heresy of a certain Tanchelijn, in my view not totally dissimilar to the Cathari, that was to survive the death of the religious agitator by many years, to be finally extirpated by St Norbert. Just as

Would ye, madam, said Sir
Launcelot, with your heart that I
were with you? Yea, truly, said
the queen. Now shall I prove my
might, said Sir Launcelot, for

Hold, said Sir Meliagrance, here is my glove that she is traitress unto my lord, King Arthur, and that this night one of the wounded knights lay with her. And I receive your glove, said Sir Launcelot.

Wolfram von Eschenbach was apparently prepared to attribute secret doctrines to the Templars, the rumour of some kind of religious revolt may have been enough for him, with his esoteric-Christian leanings, to include a reference to it in his *Parzival* with no further commentary. We get the impression that in some cases there is, if not a heretical, then at least an unorthodox substrate playing a part in the establishment of the Grail legend, and this is already the case with Chrétien.

Although it would take us too far out of the way to look closely at such aspects, von Eschenbach's mention of his spokesman Kyot-Guyod points implicitly to the Jewish astrologer Flegetanis from Toledo. Since Kyot definitely had to be from Provence, this may mean that the German poet, in line with contemporary usage, which confused or identified the two terms, actually meant a Cathar. In Provence there is still a tendency to associate the Grail tradition with its medieval Manichaeism, which had to a certain extent ousted Catholicism. This means that the citadel of Montségur has to be taken into account as a possible Grail castle and that the relic then either accompanied the romantic-heroic martyr Escarlamonde de Foix on her fiery journey to heaven or was hidden in some Pyrenean cave by her last followers, escaping from the castle just in time.

The possible contribution of the Templars to Wolfram's *Parsival* and the poet's possible spiritual links with the doctrines of the Cathari are regarded by the specialists as very doubtful. It is, however, undeniable that Wolfram deliberately, albeit distantly, wished to associate his Grail story with the Provence via Kyot-Guyod. This points to an interest in a world that was heretical by the standards of his orthodox contemporaries, or at any rate was regarded by some of them as such. He understood that he had to situate the Grail, which he represented as a precious stone with astrological or alchemical properties, outside Christian orthodoxy. When the greatest German poet of his age insists, furthermore, that he can neither write nor spell, one recognizes a ritual formula from some secret society. This pronouncement has thus far given the literary historians a lot of trouble as regards Wolfram's illiteracy or his self-deprecation, despite the obviousness of the solution offered here, which, furthermore, has a corollary in freemasonry. Wolfram set the Grail events not in Provence but, influenced by what he thought to be Master Kyot's background, in the 'other' world. With its roots reaching back to the distant past, this is effectively where the Grail belongs, despite the innocent piety of Robert de Boron and the theological balancing acts by the clever writer(s) of the prose *Lancelot*, who, writing for a wide public, probably suspected that there was more to the stories than met the eye.

We have looked in detail at the English mumming plays and related folk dances that, together with Jessie Weston, I consider to be survivals of fertility rituals that eventually led to the Arthurian romances. Everything indicates that these are exceptionally old and equally exceptionally stubborn. Using the theory of Carl-Gustav Jung, one can conceive of these as archetypal phenomena. Such phenomena amount to what some anthropologists describe as a racial memory, based on humanity's collective psychological substratum. We are not consciously aware

So in this season, as in the month of May, it befell a great anger and unhap that stinted not till the flower of chivalry of all the world was destroyed . . .

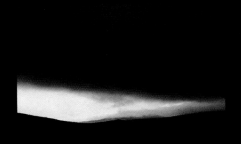

And then Sir Arthur asked them what noise they made. My lord, said Agravaine, I shall tell you that I may keep no longer. Here is I, and my brother Sir Mordred, brake unto my brothers Sir Gawaine, Sir Gaheris, and to Sir Gareth, how this we know all, that Sir Launcelot holdeth your queen, and hath done long . . .

of this but in the meantime it is passed on from generation to generation, rather like the instincts.

These structures, the archetypes, originate in the way in which primitive mortals attempt to understand and relate to the complex natural processes with which they are continually confronted. This engenders myths to explain the creation and the working of the cosmos and of life. The process began tens of thousands of years ago, which amounts to the transmission of archetypal patterns being considered as some hitherto unexplained genetic phenomenon. Even at a time when, for example, the degree of acquired rational knowledge renders myths no longer relevant to the individual or to the community, we continue to store them as a power that is ever ready to be reawakened, in the deepest, collective subconscious. We are not aware of its presence, but under the impulse of internal or external events the archetype can awaken and adapt itself, as clearly happened when the literature of Arthur and the Grail first saw the light of day.

Jessie Weston is concerned with fertility rites originating, in her view, in the Far East, and which eventually re-emerged in the Grail legends. The question, however, is whether this migration theory, applied in its most stringent form, does not make matters unnecessarily complicated. The Ice Age hunters of northern Europe relied on their own form of hunting magic, which still survives today in the English Horn Dance. From this it would appear that an unconsciously stored tradition can also be preserved in its own region, without having to come to us from the ends of the earth, where similar customs may also exist. Indeed, if the Grail tradition is possibly rooted in ancient

nature rituals, it is not necessary for these to have been imported in a roundabout way from India or anywhere else. They were part of the universal birthright of humanity and therefore belonged at the same time to the prehistory of the west.

We do not know precisely how the inhabitants of that world related to the unknown, to their gods. On the other hand, they did leave us their attempts to contact the 'other', in the form of enormous stone monuments, more widely scattered over the surface of the earth than was imagined until relatively recently.

The origin of one of these monuments is explained by Geoffrey of Monmouth in his *Historia Regum Britanniae* as follows. After a number of British chieftains had declared themselves willing to negotiate with the Saxons and had been lured by the latter into an ambush and been killed, Ambrosius Aurelianus wanted to set up a memorial to them. For this, Merlin advised him to fetch an existing famous construction, the Giant's Dance, from its site in Ireland and to set it up close to Amesbury in Wiltshire. Through Merlin's magic intervention, then, Stonehenge was built on Salisbury Plains and at the same time embedded in the Arthurian world. At the time the famous magician was performing this architectural trick, the people who, in reality, had started building Stonehenge had already got a head start on him of some 3500 years. In its final form, as still partly preserved today, it had already been standing there for 2000 years. Historically and archaeologically speaking, Geoffrey's story in this case is hopeless, which does not prevent us from looking at it more closely.

Merlin is emphatic in his attribution of magical, more particularly healing, properties to the megaliths of Stonehenge, thereby making a

[I] never gave my heart against no going, that ever ye went to the queen, so much as now; for I mistrust that the king is out this night from the queen because peradventure he hath lain some watch for you and the queen, and therefore I dread me sore of treason.

143

Truly, said the queen, I have none armour, shield, sword, nor spear; wherefore I dread me sore our long love is come to a mischievous end, for I hear by their noise there be many noble knights . . .

link with the idea of the conservation of vitality and fertility. This is apparently also bound up with the continuation of 'life' after death. Although it is never officially mentioned, the ashes of the dead have been clandestinely strewn among these stones until the present day. Furthermore, there is the remarkable fact that some of the stone blocks come from the Prescelly Mountains in South Wales. They therefore had to be transported some 200 miles by land and sea from the general direction of Ireland. I consider it possible that this may have given rise to the story of Merlin's having arranged the gigantic transfer of building materials. Although there were obviously interruptions, Stonehenge was being assembled and worked on for about 1500 years under the noses of the population of what is now Wiltshire. This would have become fixed in legends of stupendous, incomprehensible and therefore magical events, which seem to have been handed down in the form of an oral tradition with an archetypal bent as far as Geoffrey of Monmouth, who adapted it to his own literary purposes.

Archaeologists have fairly recently discovered that in about 1000 BC a road was made from the monument to the nearby river Avon, which indicates that it was in use at that time and presumably for some time after. It is surprising to realize that this agrees with one of the most perplexing texts left to us from Greek literature. This was saved by Diodorus Siculus in his *Bibliotheca Historica* (50 BC), who took it from the otherwise largely lost works of Hecataeus of Miletus (500 BC). Hecataeus himself could have had the story from tin, gold or amber traders, who were apparently regular visitors to prehistoric Wessex.

'Obliquely opposite to Celtic Gaul there is an island in the ocean, not smaller than Sicily and stretching northwards, inhabited by the Hyperboreans, who are called by that name because their home is beyond the point whence the north wind (Boreas) blows; and the land is both fertile and productive of every crop, and since it has an unusually temperate climate it produces two harvests each year. Moreover, the following legend is told concerning it: Leto was born on this island, and for that reason Apollo is honoured among them above all other gods; and the inhabitants are looked upon as priests of Apollo, after a manner, since daily they praise this god continuously in song and honour him exceedingly. And there is also on the island both a magnificent sacred precinct of Apollo and a notable temple which is adorned with many votive offerings and is spherical in shape. Furthermore, a city is there which is sacred to this god, and the majority of its inhabitants are players on the cithara; and these continually play on this instrument in the temple and sing hymns of praise to the god, glorifying his deeds . . . The account is also given that the god visits the island every nineteen years, the period in which the return of the stars to the same place in the heavens is accomplished; and for this reason the nineteen-year period is called by the Greeks the 'year of Meton'. At the time of this appearance of the god he both plays on the cithara and dances continuously the night through from the vernal equinox until the rising of the Pleiades, expressing in this manner his delight in his successes.'

Book II, Loeb Library translation

So to make short tale, they were all consented that for better outher for worse, if so were that the queen were on that morn brought to the fire, shortly they all would rescue her. And so by the advice of Sir Launcelot, they put them all in an embushment in a wood, as nigh Carlisle as they might, and there they abode still, to wit what the king would do.

Wit you well the queen was glad that she was escaped from the death. And then she thanked God and Sir Launcelot; and so he rode his way with the queen, as the French book saith, unto Joyous Gard . . .

It therefore appears that Stonehenge was dedicated to a god that the Greek writer identifies, from his customary viewpoint and therefore inevitably wrongly, as Apollo. This is, however, a meaningful error: we can in fact assume that the Stonehenge god revealed qualities corresponding to those of the Greek Apollo. Strangely enough, the latter was the sovereign lord of healing, who therefore held the threads of life and death in his hands. The related fields of youth and male beauty – he was also a renowned lover – also seem to have come under his aegis. As radiant sun god, he embodied the sun, advanced the ripening of the harvest and protected livestock. His most important act was to kill the monster Python, the dragon of the underworld and the symbol of destruction. In the Arthurian world, he is reflected to some extent in figures such as Lohengrin or, more clearly, Gawain. It is in any case reasonable to assume that Hecataeus had his information from travellers who had visited Stonehenge and had witnessed the celebratory worship of a sun god there, so that, for this period at least, the monument should be regarded as having been a sun temple.

Archaeologists will find this conclusion premature. They have always been particularly reticent about what is surely the essential question of what, in fact, this startling and architecturally unique structure was built for. It took an astronomer, Professor Gerald Hawkins, an Englishman teaching at Boston, Massachusetts, to really get down to the problem in the 1960s. He took the necessary measurements, put the collected data in an IBM computer and soon published his *Stonehenge Decoded* (1966). Summed up simply, his

conclusion is as follows. The Stonehenge construction, together with a ring of chalk-filled and therefore indelible pits, the so-called Aubrey-holes, contains the necessary data for the calculation of all possible phenomena connected with the sun and the moon, in the future as well as in the past. It is, for example, still possible today to calculate in this way on what day of any given year Easter fell or will fall. From this it appears that the prehistoric construction is a sort of giant computer.

One of the first results to perplex Hawkins was the steady repetition of a period of 18.61 years. His amazement was not due to something unknown, but to something which, as an astronomer, he was perfectly conversant with. The figure of 18.61 does in fact correspond to the Metonic cycle, so called from the discovery by the Greek astronomer Meton in the fifth century BC that 235 lunar months correspond to 19 solar years. At the end of each 19-year cycle, the phases of the moon fall again on the same days of the solar, i.e., the ordinary, calendar. An English archaeologist, R. S. Newall, later drew Hawkins' attention to the passage from Hecataeus with its reference to the 'year of Meton'. We are apparently obliged to conclude that the builders of Stonehenge had, long before Meton, been aware of this approximately 18-year cycle. This seems to have been such a great mystery to them that they linked the phenomenon to the regular appearance of their god, whose coming they presumably celebrated with great festivities on Midsummer Night (21–22 June).

Since Hecataeus refers to this god as Apollo, he was at that time already a male sun god, whatever his name may have been. This does not mean, however, that there is nothing more to be

*When this was known openly,
that King Arthur and Sir
Launcelot were at debate, many
knights were glad of their debate,
and many were full heavy of their
debate.*

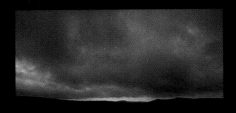

And therefore, said the king, wit you well my heart was never so heavy as it is now, and much more I am sorrier for my good knights' loss than for the loss of my fair queen; for queens I might have enow, but such a fellowship of good knights shall never be together in no company.

said. Between the time of the origins of the first, very simple form of Stonehenge and the time when the Greek writer noted the existence of the already centuries-old completed structure, is a span of about 2500 years. During this period, fundamental changes took place in the religious views of the inhabitants of western Europe. The basis for the very first monument was laid down by a population in transition from a hunting-gathering stage to that of agriculture and who still worshipped the mother-goddess. For reasons that are connected with fertility and the cyclical nature of the female reproductive system, this goddess was related not only to the life-giving earth, but also to the regularly changing phases of the moon, so that she also fulfilled the role of the white moon goddess, while Stonehenge was originally built as a moon temple and computer.

Meanwhile, Jessie Weston's concept of the migration of certain mythical notions, which I have tried to put into proportion, cannot be dismissed out of hand. Here, it is not so much a question of the migration of ideas as of the people bearing them. Generally speaking, in about 2000 BC Indo-European tribes reached the British Isles, and so, after a lengthy period of mutual influence and cultural interpenetration, shifted the emphasis from the mother-goddess, and therefore from the moon, to the sun and the father-god. In this process, the old moon temples such as Stonehenge, and possibly also the neighbouring Avebury, gradually became sun temples as well, where the rituals performed continued to enhance the fertility and general wellbeing of the people and of nature.

No one can say exactly what such rituals consisted of and what their precise purpose was. There is, on the other hand, a reasonable possibility that in communities that worship the mother-goddess we should encounter a wholly or largely matriarchal society. At the head of this there is a queen, but alongside the queen there is a prince consort, the 'ram king', whose function is to father the queen's descendants and who is then killed. Right up as far as the Grail romances, there is a discernible thread that points to a matriarchal social structure. The heroes that appear have very few ties with their fathers, who, as in Perceval's case, are usually long dead, but there is a very strong relationship between nephew and uncle, who should always be considered to be the mother's brother, indicating a typical matriarchal pattern.

Although regarded as a god in human form, it is nonetheless the prince consort or the king who, in a matriarchal society, is sacrificially killed when, at the end of a year (perhaps a Metonic year) his vital powers are thought to be on the wane, or possibly on the basis of visible symptoms of physical decline or of lack of fertility. For this horrible execution, the use of a substitute was eventually introduced and, finally, the slaughter of an animal, probably a bull, a late echo of which we find in the Spanish *corrida*. We can easily imagine that the setting for this was provided by the structures at Avebury, which is indeed regarded as a fertility temple by younger archaeologists like Michael Dames, at Stonehenge and at other stone circles, while the backdrop was provided by the Tor with its labyrinth and by the real or imaginary Glastonbury Zodiac.

In line with Jessie Weston's thinking, it would have been an event with dialogue, a sort of mystery play in a megalithic circle, comparable to Greek tragedy, in which the central ideas of the

Then came King Arthur with Sir
Gawaine with an huge host, and
laid a siege all about Joyous
Gard, both at the town and at the
castle, and there they made
strong war on both parties.

149

And all thing was made ready for their shipping to pass over the sea, and so they shipped at Cardiff. And there King Arthur made Sir Mordred chief ruler of all England . . .

Grail myth would be expressed in dramatic form, together with the relevant cult objects. The substitution of an animal for the man-god or his *locum tenens*, and the eventual, purely symbolic nature of the ancient ritual do not detract from the fact that, in the collective subconscious of the people who had observed it for centuries, the sacrifice of the king would have left the deepest mark and the strongest fixation. On the other hand, time can be said to heal archetypal wounds too, or at least soften the pain. The ritually murdered monarch became a sick one, whose cure as well as whose death could restore vitality to the barren land and reproductive power to man and beast. The original murdered demigod became the ailing Fisher-King, whose association with fish we should regard as a fertility symbol. His wound, as is clearly the case with Wolfram's Amfortas, amounts to a form of castration, sometimes caused by a sin that he has committed and which is seldom specified, but more often by the blind operations of fate. In the original mystery-ritual, various holy objects and talismans would have played a part. As mentioned earlier, two fertility symbols were the most important: a bowl, representing the vulva, and a spear, representing the male organ, later respectively the Grail and the lance. Did they perhaps once figure as sacrificial weapons, the cause of death, and as recipient to collect the victim's blood? To ask the question is to answer it.

The bits of our puzzle are gradually falling into place. After a process of transmission that lasted many hundreds of years, it is absolutely impossible to work out in detail the suggested analogy between the literature of the Round Table, which remains strongly suggestive of a megalithic circle, and prehistoric rituals. We can,

however, note that these rituals probably also involved choreographic ceremonies, on the basis of the tediously repeated folk-tale of young people singing and dancing on the Christian sabbath, whom the Lord then turned into stones. I have already suggested the hypothesis that gradually something like a mystery play developed, a primitive dramatic representation of the cycle of nature, of death and resurrection. This later left its mark on the oral folk tradition, whose mythical undercurrent can be attributed to more or less recognizable echoes of the cosmic rhythm, and this in turn led to the stories of the knights of the Round Table.

From this, the Arthurian Grail epic derived its largely confusing hermetic aspect, but occasional traces of the original rituals can nonetheless be found in the romances. Following in Jessie Weston's footsteps, we have already considered Gawain's talents as a healer. He also appears to be related to the sun, since we are told that his powers grow towards midday and wane towards evening. In the fourteenth-century English *Sir Gawain and the Green Knight*, by the rather mysterious 'Pearl poet', the prehistoric fertility ritual reveals itself in the form of a sort of beheading game. In the shape of the Green Knight, the spirit of nature is killed, but each time rises from the dead again.

The Arthurian figures with strong magical associations, like Merlin, Morgan le Fay and others, not excluding the moody and complex Kay, could usefully be analysed in the light of their obvious mythical antecedents. It is, for example, unmistakable that Mordred, as the seducer of Arthur's wife and opponent of the king, symbolizes the daemonic power that causes the downfall of the Round Table and of the

Thus as this siege endured, and as Sir Gawaine lay sick near a month; and when he was well recovered and ready within three days to do battle again with Sir Launcelot, right so came tidings unto Arthur from England that made King Arthur and all his host to remove.

And so as Sir Mordred was at Dover with his host, there came King Arthur with a great navy of ships, and galleys, and carracks. And there was Sir Mordred ready awaiting upon his landing, to let his own father to land upon the land that he was king over.

kingdom while at the same time laying waste to nature and the earlier prosperity. He is the equivalent of the mysterious opponent of St George in the mumming plays mentioned above. That the medieval writers were working with material whose original significance they no longer understood appears from the fact that Mordred was born on 1 May. He is at the same time a symbol of evil and the embodiment of summer, while his death is reminiscent of the sacrificed king. This ambiguity probably explains why, even though he represents the spirit of destruction, he is also Guinevere's lover, by implication the substitute bridegroom of both the queen and the moon goddess.

In *Perlesvaus* we see the king lose his vitality, become apathetic to the point of depression and so far jeopardize his prestige that Guinevere tries to put matters right by persuading him to engage in a highly dangerous quest. This involves a visit to a bewitched chapel in a cemetery, which automatically reminds us of the numerous burial mounds in the neighbourhood of Stonehenge. The story unfolds in such a way that at the last moment this visit does not take place, since a bold squire – a substitute in fact – goes to reconnoitre the place beforehand and is mysteriously killed. A matriarchal feature here is that Guinevere controls and manipulates events, though failing in the elaboration of an apparently sinister plan, not revealed by the author, that might have cost the life of Arthur himself. It is true that Arthur is the king, but he in fact derives his status from Guinevere's much older, matriarchal sovereignty. In the *Histoire de Fulk Fitz-Warin* (1315), the story of Arthur's expedition to the horrible chapel is told over again, only this time described as a success for

him. His fame had been sadly tarnished, but as a result of the adventure, his power is restored and he again enjoys the authority that is his due. Jessie Weston interprets this as involving a ritual journey to the realm of the dead, from which to return new-born and, in the light of prehistoric custom, presumably literally as *another* person, in the shape of a new husband for the queen.

In spite of their relative candour, we are still repeatedly left with the impression that the Christian Middle Ages did not quite know what to make of the adulterous, in their eyes plainly sinful relationship between Sir Lancelot and his queen, Guinevere. Meanwhile, the situation seems to reflect such a deeply rooted pattern that there was just no way round it, even for the most pious of poets. More than the queen's lover, the Lancelot of mythology is the substitute king. In this way he becomes in fact as important as, if not more important than, Arthur, who is already living in the psychological shadow of Avalon's eternity. Furthermore, we have the impression that Lancelot is not Guinevere's only lover. Think of the adventure with the mysterious Melwas-Maléagant, the lord of the Summer Country, who kidnaps her and, with or without her consent, sexually possesses her. Although the narrators nowhere explicitly say so, it seems that Lancelot has a number of predecessors. We are reminded here of Arthur's not only literary but presumably also historical oldest companions, namely Kay, usually represented as elderly, the dynamic Gawain, Yder, Mardoc and Caradoc, who apparently all in their turn have played the part of the substitute king.

It is difficult to escape the impression that here and there in the Arthurian romances elements appear that may indeed be indicative of an

*And there was a day assigned
betwixt King Arthur and Sir
Mordred, that they should meet
upon a down beside Salisbury,
and not far from the seaside . . .*

And when Sir Mordred felt that he had his death wound he thrust himself with the might that he had up to the bur of King Arthur's spear. And right so he smote his father Arthur, with his sword holden in both his hands, on the side of the head, that the sword pierced the helmet and the brain-pan . . .

esoteric form of Christianity from about 1200 or even considerably earlier, among whose initiates possibly a Chrétien de Troyes may be counted. Whether or not it was a figment of the Cistercians' imagination, it is a fact that primarily in the widely available prose *Lancelot* an immense importance is attached to the by now thoroughly Christianized, apparently purely orthodox Grail. Some researchers regard this as a fine and otherwise acceptable symbol for the Holy Virgin, and therefore in fact for the mother-goddess, bearing in mind that both the child Jesus and the Man of Sorrows are said to appear from it. In spite of the striking and even confusing parallel with the Eucharistic chalice, the Grail apparently reflects a more or less secret tradition, which – and this particularly has to be borne in mind – the official church always regarded with a wary eye and so never included the Grail in its iconography, however pious the tone of the relevant stories might have been.

The authorities at Glastonbury and elsewhere possibly knew or suspected more than we imagine. On the other hand, they could hardly invoke a prehistoric rite as performed at Stonehenge, Avebury and other megalithic temples and observatories under the supervision of some shaman, who was probably the indirect prototype for the figure of Merlin. Very little is known about prehistoric mythologies. There is, however, a clear present trend among a number of prehistorians and anthropologists towards regarding the arrival of new population groups, amounting to a slow, centuries-old westward drift, as not necessarily signifying a break in mythology. This has given rise to a tendency to speak of pre-Celts from about 2000 BC onwards and, even with respect to the arrival of the Celts

proper in about 800 BC, to consider the possibility of an integration of concepts and customs among the merging tribes. Meanwhile, it remains improbable that the druids, who appeared only in the last centuries before the Christian era, should have had anything to do with Stonehenge or any similar precinct. The probability is that that all began very early on, with the cosmically inspired, presumably dramatic and bloody ritual in honour of the moon-goddess from the Early Stone Age. She was identified with the queen of a matriarchal society, whose consort was sacrificed to the gods and went to join them, after which she married again in order to keep fertility at an optimum.

After centuries of lying dormant in the collective subconscious, both the queen and the sacrificed king re-emerged in the folk tradition and the literature of the Middle Ages. The moon-/mother-goddess emerged as Guinevere, whose old name was Gwenhyfaer, meaning white goddess. Alongside Guinevere there was a second survival from a matriarchal religious system in the figure of the ailing Fisher-King. He was once the monarch, in fact the prince consort, whose declining powers jeopardized the rhythm of the seasons and the vitality of nature. This was symbolized in the mythical context, possibly linked with the self-mutilation of the priests of Cybele, by an incurable wound, or even a form of castration, as appears in Wolfram von Eschenbach.

The arrival on the scene of the younger Indo-European sky god presumably created problems. He was to acquire an undeniable sovereignty over the moon-goddess, who was from then onwards regarded as his bride. This marriage, resolving the evident perturbation of the original equilibrium, was eventually reflected

Then he threw the sword as far into the water as he might; and there came an arm and an hand above the water and met it, and brandished, and then vanished away the hand with the sword in the water.

Comfort thyself, said the king, and do as well as thou mayest, for in me is no trust for to trust in; for I will into the vale of Avilion to heal me of my grievous wound: and if thou hear never more of me, pray for my soul.

in medieval literature as the marriage of Guinevere and Arthur the king. The sky god from whom he originated, however, could never completely suppress the earlier prince consort, predestined to die a sacrificial death. This explains the parallels already mentioned between Arthur and the ailing Fisher-King. In the Grail romances this also leads to the conspicuous fact that the latter remains shrouded in a highly secretive, magical or mystical context. King Arthur, who in turn is not completely free of the dangers that were once inherent in the position of the queen's husband, is in fact hero, devoid of mystery, human in his actions and predestined to die on the battlefield, in spite of his Apollonian features derived from the supreme sun god.

We are struck again and again by the amazing tenacity with which myth and legend continue to endure, with sometimes the strangest results.

Without going further into his possible mythical antecedents, we can point, for example, to a largely historical figure such as Vortigern, Geoffrey of Monmouth's arch-traitor, who on the Continent, and namely in Brittany, is remembered as Guthiern, a saint and the founder of Quimperlé in Finisterre. It is equally strange to see Sir Kay appear wearing a halo, as the patron saint of at least three Breton parishes: Saint-Quai-Portrieux, Saint-Quai-Perros and Plogoff, where he is known as Saint Ké.

Along with such place-names and completely unforeseen saints, it is interesting, since we have already mentioned the royal game of geese, to point to some curious relics in the game of chess, where the omnipotence of the queen reminds us of Guinevere, and in certain of the tarot cards (the Grail, the knight, the queen, the hanged man), which continue to evoke thoughts

associated with the Grail roman

The public of the Middle Age on folk tradition, performances talented wandering storytellers, included the Arthur stories in th and, mainly, a number of rare a costly manuscripts. Nevertheles of the knights of the Round Tab were an enormous success in the Even in our technological and le twentieth century, we are still f; them, just as our forefathers we

Superficially, we tend to attri continued attraction to the poet nature of such works, despite th exaggerated naïveté. In fact, th archetypal, underlying fundame rhythms that are part of humani birthright, reflecting the patterr death. These we carry deeply hi the collective subconscious, whi them for us when we meet them texts, even when we have no ide this mysterious fascination.

Although he obviously could himself, it was this that Sir Thor spontaneously referring to in th century when he concluded his , (about 1460) – the last but not t of the great Grail romances – w but heavily archetypal and there epitaph for his hero:

HIC JACET ARTHURUS, REX QUO FUTURUS.

In other words:

HERE LIES ARTHUR, THE ONCE /

Yet some men say in many parts of England that King Arthur is not dead, but had by the will of our Lord Jesu into another place; and men say that he shall come again, and he shall win the holy cross.

T H E   S I T E S

Abbotsbury

Glastonbury Abbey

St Michael's Mount –
Cornwall

The 'Tor' near Glastonbury

Ancient tin mine –
Bodmin Moors

Pendragon Castle – Cumbria

Dinas Bran near Llangollen

Dozmary Pool – Cornwall

Trethevy Quoit – Cornwall

Stonehenge

Avebury

Tintagel Castle

Cheesewring – Bodmin Moors

Tristan's Stone – Cornwall

Arthur's Bed – Bodmin Moors

The Hurlers – Bodmin Moors

Hill-fort near Uffington

The Round Table – Great Hall, Winchester

Raised patterns – Bossiney

Arthur's Stone – Wales

Weary-all Hill – Glastonbury

Lion's Quoit – Cornwall

Men-an-tol – Cornwall

The text editions of the Arthurian romances mentioned in this book are not listed in the bibliography. These works are available in most western European languages in a range of standard editions, as well as in generally well-explained (paperback) editions for easier reading, or even in reasonably reliable popular versions. Compendia and other specialized or general works of reference consulted in the course of writing the book have similarly not been listed.

ALCOCK, LESLIE, *Arthur's Britain*, Allen Lane-The Penguin Press, London 1971.

ALCOCK, LESLIE, *By South Cadbury is that Camelot*, Thames and Hudson, London 1972.

ANDERSON, J. R. L., *The Oldest Road, The Exploration of the Ridgeway*, Wildwood House, London 1975.

ASHE, GEOFFREY, *King Arthur's Avalon*, Collins-Fontana Books, Godalming 1957.

ASHE, GEOFFREY, *Avalonian Quest*, Methuen, London 1982.

ASHE, GEOFFREY, *Camelot and the Vision of Albion*, Panther, St Albans 1975.

ASHE, GEOFFREY, *The Quest for Arthur's Britain*, Pall Mall Press, London 1969.

ASHE, GEOFFREY, *A Guidebook to Arthurian Britain*, Longman, London 1980.

ASHE, GEOFFREY, *The Glastonbury Tor Maze*, Foot of the Tree, Glastonbury 1979.

ASHTON, GRAHAM, *The Realm of King Arthur*, Newport (Wight) 1974.

BARBER, RICHARD, *Arthur of Albion. An Introduction to the Arthurian Literature and Legends of England*, Boydell Press, London 1961.

BARBER, RICHARD, *King Arthur in Legend and History*, Cardinal, London 1973.

BARLOW, FRANK, *The Feudal Kingdom of England, 1042–1216*, Longman, London 1955.

BEDA, *A History of the English Church and People*, Penguin Books, Harmondsworth (Middlesex) 1972.

BULLEID, ARTHUR, *The Lake Villages of Somerset*, Glastonbury Antiquarian Society, Glastonbury 1980.

CAVENDISH, ROBERT, *King Arthur and the Grail*, Weidenfeld and Nicolson, London 1978.

CHADWICK, NORA K., *Celtic Britain*, Thames and Hudson, London 1963.

CHADWICK, NORA K. and DILLON, MYLES, *The Celtic Realms*, Weidenfeld and Nicolson, London 1967.

DAMES, MICHAEL, *The Great Silbury Treasure: The Great Goddess Rediscovered*, Thames and Hudson, London 1976.

DAMES, MICHAEL, *The Avebury Cycle*, Thames and Hudson, London 1977.

DAVENSON, HENRI, *Les Troubadours*, Éditions du Seuil, Paris 1961.

DEACON, RICHARD, *John Dee*, Frederick Müller, London 1968.

DOBSON, C. C., *Did Our Lord visit Britain as they say in Cornwall and Somerset?*, Covenant Publishing Co., London 1967.

DUVAL, PAUL-MARIE, *Les Celtes*, NRF-Gallimard, Paris 1977.

DUXBURY, BRENDA, etc. *King Arthur Country in Cornwall: In Search of the Real Arthur*, Bossiney Books, St Teath, Bodmin (Cornwall) 1978.

—, *Folklore, Myths and Legends of Britain*, Readers' Digest Association, London 1973.

FOX, AILEEN, *South West England*, Thames and Hudson, London 1964.

FRAZER, JAMES GEORGE, *The Golden Bough*, Macmillan-St Martin's Press, London-New York 1966.

GALLAIS, PIERRE, *Perceval et l'initiation*, Les Éditions du Sirac, Paris 1972.

GANTZ, JEFFREY, *The Mabinogion*, Penguin Books, Harmondsworth (Middlesex) 1982.

GEOFFREY OF MONMOUTH, *The History of the Kings of Britain*, Penguin Books, Harmondsworth (Middlesex) 1966.

GERALD OF WALES, *The Journey through Wales/The Description of Wales*, Penguin Books, Harmondsworth (Middlesex) 1978.

GIMBUTAS, MARIJA, *The Gods and Goddesses of Old Europe*, 7000–3500 BC, Thames and Hudson, London 1974.

GRAVES, ROBERT, *The White Goddess*, Faber & Faber, London 1957.

GREED, JOHN A., *Glastonbury Tales*, St Trillo Publications, Portishead (Bristol) 1975.

HAWKINS, GERALD S., *Stonehenge Decoded*, Fontana-Collins, London 1972.

HIBBERT, CHRISTOPHER, *The Search for King Arthur*, Cassell, London 1970.

HUNT, ROBERT, *Cornish Folk-lore*, Tor Mark Press, Truro n.d.

JENKINS, ELISABETH, *The Mystery of King Arthur*, Michael Joseph Ltd, London 1975.

JOHNSON, STEPHEN, *Roman Fortification on the 'Saxon Shore'*, Department of Environment, Her Majesty's Stationery Office, London 1977.

JOWETT, GEORGE F., *The Drama of the Lost Disciples*, Covenant, London 1970.

JUNG, EMMA and FRANZ M. L. VON, *Die Graalslegende in Psychologischer Sicht*, Rascher Verlag, Zürich-Stuttgart 1950.

LOOMIS, ROGER SHERMAN, *The Grail, from Celtic Myth to Christian Symbol*, University of Wales Press, Cardiff 1963.

LOOMIS, ROGER SHERMAN, *Arthurian Literature in the Middle Ages, A Collaborative History*, Clarendon Press, Oxford 1969.

LOTH, J., *Les Mabigonion*, Otto Zeller, Osnabrück 1969.

MALTWOOD, KATHLEEN E., *A Guide to Glastonbury's Temple of the Stars*, James Clarke & Co., London 1964.

MARKALE, JEAN, *La Roi Arthur et la Société Celtique*, Payot, Paris 1976.

MARALE, JEAN, *Les Celtes et la Civilisation Celtique*, Payot, Paris 1973.

MARKALE, JEAN, *La Tradition Celtique et Bretagne Armoricaine*, Payot, Paris 1975.

MARKALE, JEAN, *La Femme Celte*, Payot, Paris 1972.

MARKALE, JEAN, *Aliénor d'Aquitanie*, Payot, Paris 1979.

MARK, JEAN, *La légende Arthurienne et le Graal*, Presses Universitaires de France, Paris 1952.

MEYER, R., *Het Mysterie van de Graal*, W. de Haan, Zeist 1952.

MIERLO, JOZEF VAN, *Jacob van Maerlant*, Koninklijke Vlaamse Academie voor Taal- en Letterkunde, Gent 1943.

MORRIS, JOHN, *The Age of Arthur*, Weidenfeld & Nicolson, London 1973.

NELLI, RENE, *Lumière du Graal*, Les Cahiers du Sud, Paris 1951.

OWEN, D. D. R., *The Evolution of the Grail Legend*, Oliver and Boyd, London 1968.

PERNOUD, REGINE, *Aliénor d'Aquitanie*, Albin Michel, Paris 1965.

PIGGOTT, STUART, *The Druids*, Thames and Hudson, London 1968.

POWELL, T. G. E., *The Celts*, Thames and Hudson, London 1958.

RAHN, OTTO, *Kreuzzug gegen den Gral*, H. E. Günther Verlag, Stuttgart 1964.

REISER, OLIVER L., *This Holyest Erthe, the Glastonbury Zodiac and King Arthur's Camelot*, Perennial Books, London 1974.

RIVOALLAN, A., *Présence des Celtes*, Nouvelle Librairie Celtique, Paris n.d.

ROWBOTHAN, JOHN FREDERICK, *The Troubadours and Courts of Love*, Swann Sonneschein & Co., London 1895.

RUPP, HEINZ, *Wolfram von Eschenbach*, Wissenschaftliche Buchgesellschaft, Darmstadt 1966.

SAKLATVALA, BERAM, *Arthur, Roman Britain's Last Champion*, David and Charles, Newton Abbot 1971.

SCHUETZE, ALFRED, *Mithras, Mysterien und Urchristentum*, Urachhaus, Stuttgart 1972.

SCOUEZEC, GWENC'HLAN LE, *Guide de la Bretagne mystérieuse*, Tchou, Paris 1966.

SENIOR, MICHAEL, *Myths of Britain*, Orbis Publishing, London 1979.

SHARKEY, JOHN, *Celtic Mysteries*, Thames and Hudson, London 1975.

SMITHETT, LEWIS LIONEL, *St Joseph of Arimathea at Glastonbury*, James Clarke & Co., London 1964.

SPENCE, LEWIS, *The Mysteries of Britain*; The Aquarian Press, London 1970.

TREHARNE, R. F., *The Glastonbury Legends*, Sphere Books Ltd, London 1971.

VRIES, JAN DE, *La Religion des Celtes*, Payot, Paris 1975.

WAITE, ARTHUR EDWARD, *The Hidden Church of the Holy Grail*, Rebman, London 1909.

WESTON, JESSIE L., *From Ritual to Romance*, Doubleday Anchor Books, New York 1957.

WILLIAMS, MARGARET, *The Pearl Poet*, Random House, New York 1970.

WOELDEREN, HELENE W. VAN, *Waren Jesus und Joseph von Arimathia in England?* Selbstverlag Missionsbuch Wortgemeinde, Dachsbach-Rauschenberg 1975.

WRIGHT, DUDLEY, *Druidism, the Ancient Faith of Britain*, E.P. Publishing Ltd, Wakefield 1974.